Advance praise for
Demystifying Awakening

"With skill and compassion, Stephen invites a surrendering into the formless, luminous presence that is our true home. This is a rich and beautiful resource for those called to deepen their exploration of Awakening and freedom."

—**Tara Brach, best-selling author of *Trusting the Gold* and *Radical Compassion***

"We all long for a timeless inner peace—and Stephen Snyder shows us the path to it. As a guide, he is friendly, helpful, and sweetly encouraging. In his pages, you feel like you're coming home to who you've always been: wakeful, loving, contented, and wise. He's done a brilliant job of clearing away the clutter and summarizing the essential steps of full Awakening. It's a joy to walk them!"

—**Rick Hanson, PhD, *NYT* best-selling author of *Neurodharma* and *Buddha's Brain***

"A unique and profound manual. It clearly and succinctly unveils the path and process of Awakening as practiced, lived, and taught by Stephen Snyder. Written from deep experiential knowledge and wisdom, this book resonates as a transmission of Awakening."

—**Judson Brewer, MD, PhD, *NYT* best-selling author of *Unwinding Anxiety* and *The Craving Mind***

"A remarkable grounding in the Absolute—in the formless, timeless, spaceless reality that is always immediately with us, showing up as every moment of our lives—radiates right through this deeply compassionate work. It maps out, compares, and shares the paths to profound Awakening that the author has trod himself, making the paths seem accessible to each and every one of us—as in fact they are. There is indeed a path to Awakening—or even 84,000 paths—and accepting Stephen's invitation to join him on the deep ones presented here will surely be the journey of a lifetime."

—**Henry Shukman, author of *One Blade of Grass* and guiding teacher of Mountain Cloud Zen Center**

"Stephen has written a profound manual of Awakening that is rich with the insights of a lifetime of practice, and abundant with the kinds of insights that can only come from the firsthand experience of one who has truly walked the path. A must read for everyone who is serious about waking up in this life!"

—**Steve James, educator, founder of the Movement Koan Method, and host of the *Guru Viking Podcast***

"In *Demystifying Awakening*, Stephen Snyder pulls back the curtain on the process and experiences of spiritual Awakening. He offers a gradual and multifaceted series of practices, including self-inquiry, meditation, and contemplation, derived from his own practice and from his years of guiding and supporting others. This is not a conceptual book for scholars; rather, it's a book for those of us who long for the freedom that the Buddha promised and who are willing to walk the walk."

—**Jennifer Wheeler, MA, Buddhist Studies, University of Sunderland**

"If you've been on the hunt for a practical guide to dissolving the small self and its many-colored coat of suffering, stop here. In *Demystifying Awakening*, Stephen deconvolutes and disambiguates the many steps and stages of enlightenment, grounding even the wordless, formless, ageless, entirely empty realm-that-is-not-a-realm into right-now possibility. He walks you right to the edge."

—Elizabeth Koch, founder of Unlikely Collaborators

"To say I've been waiting—throughout fifty years of Buddhist practice—for someone to write this book is an understatement. Finally, here is a presentation of the path to Awakening, the processes of growth, and how to address the obstacles within the unfolding of insight and realization. It carefully lays out the methods for breaking through the barriers of self-identity to Awakening, and provides descriptions and confirmation of the awakened state. This book is a guide, a manual, a companion to any practitioner in retreat or on the path to Awakening."

—Dhammadasa, founder and former director of Cloud Mountain Retreat Center

"*Demystifying Awakening* is enormous in its scope, from the beginning of practice to expansive experiences of Awakening. To condense a lifetime journey into a book is an incredible undertaking and results in a gift to those who can find themselves somewhere in its pages. It is clear that the book is offered as an inspiration and encouragement to the practitioner, and in this it succeeds completely."

—Susie Harrington, meditation teacher at Desert Dharma

"Stephen lovingly guides us through the subtle landscapes of the Awakening process, inviting us to know for ourselves our true identity. He does this with precision, rigor, and the felt sense of direct realization. This book transmits a depth of nuanced wisdom that is rare."

—**Marisa Mohrer, LMSW, MPH, trauma therapist and author of** *Songs of Awakening*

"*Demystifying Awakening* is an immediate classic! This book clarifies and explains the core principles and teachings of the spiritual journey to Awakening. This book consolidates Stephen's years of experience in meditation, Awakening, and teaching; it is a must read for anyone who has ever had an interest in discovering a deeper truth."

—**Ñānavira, Matthew Buckley, Buddhist monk**

"A wonderful guide to the Awakening path. Lucid and precise, Stephen shares his story of the precious gift of his own Awakening through Buddhist teachings and practices. I recommend this book to anyone interested in the path of Awakening in any tradition as well as to followers of Buddhist practices."

—**Constance Corson, MD, psychiatrist and meditation teacher**

"Stephen's direct experiences of *jhāna*, emptiness, and Awakening—coupled with his ability to transmit these experiences through his teaching and writing—are extraordinary. This book is well worth having in everyone's library."

—**Warren Buck, PhD, physicist and meditation teacher**

Demystifying
Awakening

Demystifying Awakening

A Buddhist Path of Realization,

Embodiment, and Freedom

STEPHEN SNYDER

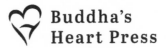 **Buddha's**
Heart Press

Buddha's Heart Press
awakeningdharma.org
Midland, MI, USA

Library of Congress Control Number: 2021924389
ISBN: 978-1-7347810-6-9 (hardcover)
ISBN: 978-1-7347810-5-2 (e-book)

Editing by Erin Parker
Proofreading by Lynn Slobogian
Cover and interior design by Jazmin Welch
E-book production by Bright Wing Media
Project management by Carra Simpson

*I dedicate this book to my Guamanian mother
who raised me for the first seven years of my life.
From her I learned the invaluable lessons of
giving and receiving unconditioned love
and of seeing nature as teacher.*

Contents

Introduction

A CORNERSTONE OF BUDDHISM, Awakening is seeing clearly through the lens of who we take ourselves to be in quiet recognition of our abiding **true nature**. True nature is the absence of a separate self, coupled with a direct knowing of the unbreakable connection, of Oneness, of all life, including each of us as our true nature. Approximately 2,600 years ago, Shakyamuni Buddha awoke from the conceptual conviction that he (and every other living being) was only a separate individual. The Buddha's deep Awakening was revolutionary. His customary **self-identity** fell away never to return. He maneuvered through life appearing as a human in earthly form while internally his **awareness** was resting in and as the source of all life, the **Absolute realm**.

Awakening includes seeing the many wholesome qualities of our true identity, our true nature. These inherent qualities include unconditioned love, **innate goodness**, profound stillness of peace, complete welcoming acceptance, mutual joy, deep compassion, wholesome strength, uncon-ditioned support, and pristine clarity, to name just a few.

From my perspective there are three components to an experience of Awakening:

1 A deep experience of **absence of self**
2 A life-altering experience of seeing one's true nature
3 A thorough unity experience where all is one or everything is a fabric of Oneness

The depth of an Awakening experience is marked by how long the Awakening experience lasts (i.e., minutes versus weeks) and how thoroughly the conviction in the separate me is dislodged, short term as well as long term.

Demystifying Awakening is a practice manual for those who feel an inescapable inner fire to wake up to ultimate truth, ultimate reality. Not conventional truths but, rather, the deepest objective universal truths, which reveal who we really are, how the world actually works, how to embody and live from the depths of and as the mysterious unconditioned qualities of our true nature.

This book not only presents and demystifies the process of Awakening, but it also engages in time-tested meditations and practices that orient our consciousness to the infinity of our source. As a meditation and spiritual practitioner, your function is to fan this inner flame to realize, embody, and express the deepest truths of creation until you and your entire world are thoroughly consumed by the fire of truth that vanquishes untruth—until indestructible, unconditioned true nature arises from the flames of inner truth revealing who we always were and always will be.

Before we dive in, I would like to explore what awakens and where Awakening takes our consciousness. We each hold deep, unquestioned, core conceptual convictions about how the world works and who we are in this world. We can hold the customary self-identity who we take ourselves to be, as unquestionably as we hold the concept of gravity. We do not need to spend time debating gravity among ourselves. We view gravity and our self-identity as unquestioned reality. This is where we are landed when we start a journey of Awakening. We then begin gradually questioning the truth of our self-identity by regularly entering meditation and closely observing our behavior for incongruities. Through the process of Awakening practices, we begin to see what was unconscious within and invite what was unknown into the light of truth. In one moment, our lives and world change. When we enter the Awakening process through either an absence of self or an inclusive dive into unconditioned love/innate goodness, our mental and physical self-identity temporarily fall away revealing what is indestructible in our awareness and consciousness. Relief overwhelms us. The peace, the love, the goodness, the truth of all reality was always right outside our view. Now we not only know it, it begins to land in our consciousness giving rise to behavior in accord with the deepest truths of the universe.

When our consciousness awakens to its ever-present connection to the deepest truth—that we are a unique, precious manifestation of unconditioned love, of innate goodness—we can deeply relax and trust the benevolence of the universe. We are at ease; finally, we are home.

> *When our consciousness awakens to its ever-present connection to the deepest truth, . . . we are at ease; finally, we are home.*

Returning Home

At the source of the universe, the center of all reality, is what we call in Buddhism **nibbāna** or *nirvāṇa*. *Nibbāna* is the ceasing of all materiality and mentality. It is the direct experience of the Absence quality of the Absolute realm, what can be called the Ninth *Jhāna* in Buddhism. *Nibbāna* is an experience of complete acceptance and complete surrender that is a potential realization on a spiritual path. **Cessation** is the quiet, still center of the Absolute realm, a realm filled with unconditioned love, innate goodness, pure **presence**, and pure awareness. The experience of Cessation occurs in the unmanifest side of the Absolute realm, the Ninth *Jhāna*. The unmanifest side is a richly dark, expansive, nonconceptual realm with Absence of everything. The manifest side of the Absolute realm contains a nearly blinding brightness of pure unconditioned love, innate goodness, pure presence/beingness, and pure awareness.

In the experience of Cessation, our awareness will first pass through a field—an energy—of generative, unconditioned, all-accepting love; untarnished goodness; all-inclusive presence; and deeply penetrating awareness. It is a full, complete presence of **Beingness**. It is a satisfying love that soothes and eases; we rest in the buoyancy, the okayness, that opens us to completely trust exactly where we are. We contact the trust, the knowing, that innate goodness will always triumph over unhealthy, destructive behavior. Consistent contact with our true nature can confirm there is always a basis for optimism and good expectations in the world and in our lives. It is a love and goodness that have a **felt sense** of profound potency, like a seed planted and nourished in your garden by warm sun and gentle rain that has ripened to the point that it is poised to burst forth out of its earthly home into the brilliant sunlight and nourishing fresh air.

This field of potent, all-accepting, unconditioned love and innate goodness is what I call the Absolute realm. I use the term "**Absolute**" to convey it is an inclusive reality that has no conditions or conceptual partitions. It is not born and does not die. Thus, it is unconditioned and, most importantly, is always present and available in this moment, in every moment. Contacting and abiding in the Absolute realm allows our consciousness to rest in a unified field of deep all-accepting love, deep presence, and profound warmth that welcomes us home. In a theistic religion, the Absolute realm would be equivalent to God. It is the animating source of all life with complete, unconditioned, unending, welcoming acceptance. Everything we are and we can reference about ourselves is welcomed. There is no behavior nor way of being that will be rejected by the Absolute realm. You are and will be welcome when you return home despite any guilt or shame you may hold as identity.

As our consciousness is drawn deeper into the dark mysterious quality of the Absolute realm, we will notice that our thoughts, and the functioning of closely held concepts of self-identity, dramatically slow. Any sense or marker of a me—through referencing our body, our inner narrative, our likes and dislikes—begins to be enveloped in a welcome, stunningly profound silence. Imagine it as the silence of deep space. Our consciousness begins to merge back into the most significantly profound silence that can possibly be imagined. We gratefully release and surrender all control from within as we are enveloped into our source. It feels like the warm, inviting womb of the universe, the origin of all life and the source, perfectly satisfying our soul's deepest longing. At some point as we are drawn deeper into our source—the Absolute realm—consciousness and awareness stop. They cease. Expansive, enveloping absence is the all-inclusive reality in this experience of Cessation. It is the halting of every marker of mental or physical identity. Any way you can know yourself or reference any self ends.

It is only after the experience in Cessation ceases, as our consciousness begins to drift back toward the generatively loving goodness of the Absolute realm, that we become cognizant. When our consciousness and awareness reactivate following the experience of Cessation, we also discover fruition consciousness—a grounded, direct, intuitive understanding that our sense of self, our identity itself, our locus of perception has changed. This direct knowledge then reveals the impact, the spiritual or meditative fruit, of such a merging of individual awareness with universal awareness. Awareness is never two, nor is it one. It is without concept.

Awareness is once again resting in pure, enveloping, all-accepting love; innate goodness; and all-inclusive presence. It is a sparklingly transcendent love that welcomes all without differentiation, without any preference as to any form or asserting any function of rejection. We know and feel the deep acceptance of all-encompassing love and pure innate goodness. We not only feel whole—we feel effortlessly embraced and nourished in a place, a realm, in which we completely belong. We know, with absolute certainty and complete conviction, we are home. Home is us.

While home is always near, we cannot perceive or experience it without spiritual work, as it is covered behind the bank of clouds of our conceptual convictions defining reality. That is, the deepest truth we believe in before Awakening is that we are a separate individual whose success or failure is tied exclusively to our effort alone. We begin with meditations and practices that orient our awareness toward qualities of our deeper or true nature as we gently question and slightly challenge our conceptual convictions. Our conceptual convictions and deep beliefs in a separate self are revealed as hollow through the process and experience of Awakening. This is our journey.

Paths to a First Awakening

A **First Awakening**, in my experience, includes both an experience of unity, of all is One or One is all, and a deep experience of absence of the customary self-identity along with an identification with our deepest or true nature. So, practically speaking, there is an absence of the customary self-identity, the recognition of true nature as our true identity, and the coemerging experience of a loving Oneness that completely envelops all.

There is no way to predict when any one person will have a First Awakening experience. Nonetheless, we can participate in foundational meditations and spiritual practices that till the soil and fertilize the ground for the young shoot of Awakening to emerge. There are a number of paths to First Awakening and from there to the fully functioning self-realization called *nibbāna/nirvāṇa* in Buddhism. The three main paths I am familiar with are the path of insight, the path of absorption or *jhāna*, and the path of heart.

The path of insight is well presented in the book *Manual of Insight* by Mahāsi Sayadaw, so I will not be presenting that path in this book.

Foundational meditations and spiritual practices till the soil and fertilize the ground for the young shoot of Awakening to emerge.

The path of *jhāna* is well explained in *Practicing the Jhānas*, which I coauthored. In the *jhāna* path, you are developing **concentration meditation** to the level of absorption or *jhāna*. This is a very high level of meditative concentration where, after concentrating on a specific singular meditative object, your sense of self quiets and becomes temporarily transparent. Thoughts fade, and pleasant, wholesome, unconditioned feeling states of joy, bliss, and one-pointedness arise as support for the deepening. In the *jhāna* path, typically one commences with *ānāpānasati* or breath awareness meditation. This can be developed through the first four form *jhānas*. These are called form *jhānas* as there is a purification of our form, meaning our perception of being a solid, separate, individual body. From the Fourth *Jhāna*, one would use a *kasina*, which is a mind-made meditative object, to journey through each of the four form *jhānas* and potentially enter the four formless *jhānas*/realms.

The formless or upper *jhānas*/realms are the Base of Boundless Space (the Fifth *Jhāna*), the Base of Boundless Consciousness (the Sixth *Jhāna*), the Base of No-thing-ness (the Seventh *Jhāna*), and the Base of Neither Perception nor Non-perception (the Eighth *Jhāna*). From the Eighth *Jhāna* concentration experience, it is possible to access a secret teaching presented as the Ninth *Jhāna*, what I call the Absolute realm. This is the source of no-source, the generative aliveness that animates all life force.

While the *jhāna* path is a viable path to journey through mind states as well as rarified states of **consciousness**, it is not a path that is readily accessible to most people. That is one reason I prefer to start students on a path with heart, which is the path I will be explaining and detailing in this book. After a deep realization of **no-self** or a First Awakening, I introduce *jhāna* practice through the heart meditations called the *brahmavihāras*.

In the path of heart, we can journey from contact with our innate goodness—a quality of our deeper or true nature—to a deep, penetrating merging into and as the Absolute realm and its qualities of universal love, innate goodness, pure Presence, and absence of self. The beginning and end, the alpha and omega of the universe as we know and experience it is unconditioned universal love. Love is the generative flow, the core, the heart essence, of all of life. Universal love is a tender and loving presence. It is the source of all states of consciousness, as well as the origin of everything. When the loving presence of universal love is seen as our true nature—the essence, the life force, of everything that exists—the universe is unshakably known to be benevolent and trustworthy.

When we are resting in loving presence, we feel held by the universe, attended to with remarkable attunement, and taken care of in a loving, appropriate way. Most importantly we feel loved unconditionally by and through direct contact with our Beingness itself. Universal love can be experienced as soft, gentle, intricate, sweet, and beautifully delicate. It gives us a sense that we can trust the rightness and inherent truth of the presence of the universe and everything will be more than okay.

Demystifying Awakening: A Buddhist Path of Realization, Embodiment, and Freedom is a continuation of my book *Buddha's Heart*. In *Buddha's Heart*, I explain, present, and detail the ancient Buddhist heart practices and meditations. In this book I will be continuing with the heart practices and meditations with an aim toward helping readers open to a First Awakening, deepen self-realization, and experience Cessation/*nibbāna*/*nirvāṇa*. This journey of Awakening will involve embodying our realizations and working on the incongruent parts of our psyche and customary self-identity, while living from our deepest truth.

This book is offered as an explanation of the whole of the spiritual path from the perspective of awakeness and is structured to reflect this. There are conceptual presentations to demystify and help the reader understand the path of Awakening. Also included are practices and meditations that support awareness—drawing consciousness deeper into ultimate reality, toward the source of all realities—and practical suggestions to assist the embodiment and lived expression of realization.

Following this introduction, which concludes with my First Awakening experience and foundational practices for a path of Awakening, we turn first to "Orientation and Preparation," a chapter that contains a discussion of central terms and concepts such as "self," "*dukkha* (unsatisfactoriness)," "absence of self," and "no-self."

In the chapter called "Awakening," we then explore the Zen path of Awakening and the **Theravada** stages of Awakening to better understand how Buddhism has conceptually oriented meditative experiences of Awakening. The focus of much of the Zen tradition is Awakening itself, and its map of Awakening has a directness and simplicity in its presentation. The Zen map tracks more closely my direct experiences and my students'. Yet, the Theravada map of

Awakening is the original map of Buddhism and Awakening. For this reason, it is helpful to understand how it lays out the stages. At the end of this chapter is a selection of processes and practices that support Awakening. I believe that as the concepts and beliefs of Awakening are explained and unpacked, the reality of these experiences can more thoroughly land in an individual's consciousness.

The next chapter, *"Pāramīs/*Character Development," is both an introduction to the Buddhist perfections of behavior, which can be explored, understood, and implemented at all stages of the path, and an invitation to observe and investigate incongruent behavior that highlights when and how we are out of sync with our spiritual intentions and practice goals. As we evolve toward behaving in greater congruence with our spiritual understanding, we more closely walk our talk—that is, live our life with our outside matching our inside, our inner knowing. As we reorient our behavior to be more aligned with our spiritual understanding, we have fewer karmic blocks to Awakening, and we do less harm in the totality of our lives. There are exercises related to generosity (*dāna*), wholesomeness/virtue (*sīla*), renunciation (***nekkhamma***), wisdom (***paññā***), energy (***vīriya***), patience (***khanti***), truthfulness (***sacca***), resolve (***adhiṭṭhāna***), loving-kindness (*mettā*), and equanimity (*upekkhā*).

As its title suggests, the final chapter of the book focuses on deepening realizations, including the formless realms and the Absolute realm, and culminates in the experience of source merging completely with source—*nirodha samādhi* (Cessation). In addition, after a number of self-realizations, it is possible for the diamondlike—luminous, indestructible—body of consciousness called the ***Vajra*** **body** to be realized. The *Vajra* body is what transmits self-realizations from lifetime to lifetime in rebirth.

With instructions for practices and exercises for readers of all experience levels, this book is suitable for those who are new on a spiritual path and for those with decades of meditation and spiritual practice experience. For ease of reference, you will also find at the end of this book a glossary of key terms that appear frequently in these pages (each term appears in bold the first time it is used in the book). I welcome every sincere spiritual student to walk this path of Awakening, a wonderous journey with breathtaking vistas.

My First Awakening

Imagine a vast ocean with waves slowly moving across the surface heading for a distant shoreline. The ocean is our source and each of us is a wave on this ocean. The ongoing experience of seeing our wave altered by wind, rain, and changes in the ocean leads us to reasonably conclude our wave is connected to but separate from the ocean. In an Awakening experience we deeply realize we are the wave and the wave is all ocean. Yet following a First Awakening, we return to a conceptual belief in the independence of the wave despite knowing deeply that our wave is actually ocean. With deepening self-realizations, we loosen and release the conceptual convictions supporting our separation from ocean until ocean is ocean and ocean is wave at once.

In a First Awakening (**kenshō**) we realize that the wave is sometimes ocean. In a **satori** experience the realization is that ocean is always wave. In a **Daigo-tettei** realization, we deeply know that ocean is ocean, ocean is wave, and wave is ocean, always. *Kenshō*, *satori*, and *Daigo-tettei* are terms I will define more fully in the section on the Zen model of Awakening (see pages 102–120).

> *Imagine a vast ocean with waves slowly moving across the surface heading for a distant shoreline. . . . In an Awakening experience we deeply realize we are the wave and the wave is all ocean.*

It will be useful for our exploration of the path into First Awakening—through the deepest realms of self-realization and the embodiment of these self-realizations—to witness and understand what a First Awakening can look like. This is the story of mine, shared to normalize the experience for others.

I began a daily meditation practice in the Zen Buddhist tradition in 1976 while reading the landmark book *The Three Pillars of Zen* by Roshi Philip Kapleau. My first meditation practice was a concentration practice of counting breaths. I counted them at the tip of my nose. The first inhalation was 1 and the first exhalation was 2. I would count as high as possible while staying as thoroughly focused on my breath as possible for a nineteen-year-old with slight attention deficit.

When I began daily meditation in 1976, I did not reveal my meditation practice to anyone. I suppose I was concerned others would not take my burgeoning meditation practice as seriously as I did. I did not know anyone else with a meditation practice whom I could share this with. That was how rare it was at the time. About a year into my meditation practice, people I knew, mostly from work, began to tell me how calm and patient I had become. Since I was primarily focused on the struggles in my personality patterning, I was not tracking the subtle positive changes that were taking place within. I attended my first Zen seven-day retreat around this time. It was a very difficult retreat that involved meditating for ten or more hours a day. I took the Buddhist precepts at that time, officially becoming a Zen Buddhist. (The Buddhist precepts are similar to Christianity's Ten Commandments. The precepts are not commandments from God but, rather, an expression of a realized life.) Other than at this one retreat, I did not work with a teacher during this time.

During the next nine years I continued to diligently meditate, generally sitting in meditation at least twice a day. I was also having inner flashes of intuitive knowing of my true nature during these years. These experiences did not really change me yet confirmed the potential fruits of the meditations.

In 1987, I was a twenty-nine-year-old attorney who was married with two children under the age of five. Despite the many demands on my time, I continued to meditate at least ninety minutes a day.

In the course of my self-education on Buddhism and Zen in particular, I was reading whatever I could lay my hands on in English. In the process of reading *The Sixth Patriarch's Dharma Jewel Platform Sutra* by Sixth Patriarch Hui-neng and with commentary by Tripitaka Master Hua, I came upon a line from another sutra entitled *The Diamond Sutra*. (The Diamond, or *Vajra* as it is called in Buddhism, is the indestructible and timeless quality of our awake consciousness containing all realizations and essential knowing.) The line was "Produce the thought that is nowhere supported." When I first read that line, I felt gobsmacked. Something grabbed me. I was tangled up with this particular line of the sutra. I could not solve its riddle. I was unable to fully pick it up or effectively put it down. The line "Produce the thought that is nowhere supported" was on unending repeat in my mind. No matter what I did or what I thought, this line would constantly assert itself. I could not solve the puzzle of what this line from the sutra meant.

I began to meditate in every free moment of my day or night. Every breath I took was "Produce the thought that is nowhere supported." I continued in this fashion for a few weeks, maybe even a few months.

As I was unable to solve this riddle deeply lodged in my consciousness, I decided to use a logical approach to figure it out. I began with one of my five senses: sight. Starting with my eye, I began to meditatively and intuitively trace back where sight began. I saw bare perception, pure awareness, without any knowing or meaning. What was seen were objects of light and shadow. I then traced sight to the optic nerve. This was the mechanics of sight but did not resolve my personal *kōan*.

Then I moved my awareness from the optic nerve to the brain. I could understand that bare perception/pure awareness travelled to the brain where it was compared to memories and experiences to try to find a match or similarity. I was seeking the location where meaning was added to bare perception. Despite my sincere and dedicated exploration, I could not find a me, an inner source of sight. I was not controlling either the bare perception nor the meaning of that bare perception.

When I arrived at the source of sight, which was a particular place in the brain, I confirmed there was no me, no doer, at the controls operating the sense field of sight. I intuitively placed a mental marker at the source of sight. I did the same practice of marking the brain's source for each of the remaining four senses.

The final sense I traced back was sound. I started with the raw data of vibration reaching my ear. I traced its source up the hearing canal to the part of the brain that must control and interpret sound. Once again, I found no me operating this sense. When my awareness and intuition arrived simultaneously at the source of sound, I arrived at the intersection of each of the other senses and the four intuitive markers previously placed by me. When I went to place the fifth mental marker, I deeply saw that I was not there! I was not here! Not only was there no me directing the source of the five senses, there was no me at all, anywhere!

Seeing there was no me was a shock to my system. I was completely dumbfounded, excited, and relieved. I was dumbfounded because I had learned to believe the social messages that there is most definitely a me running my life, mind, and body. I was excited and relieved to let go of all the ways I tried to remind myself that I was this particular me. It felt like putting down a heavy boulder I had been carrying most of my life while trying to convince myself the boulder was who I was. I was excited by being with an undeniable truth—I did not exist!

Rather than being an upsetting or perplexing experience, it was an enormous relief. I was not in charge. There was no me doing anything! It felt as though my consciousness, my soul, exhaled fully all the pent-up anxiety about what I could see was strictly a concept—that I was the doer of my life. I was not the doer. There was no doer. There had never been a doer. It was a profound relief to witness the whole of reality be in its place rather than where I conceptually held all of reality. For example, a tree could be a tree, not a leaf-shedding nuisance, to me. Its meaning was not dependent upon my relationship or reactivity to the object of perception. A mountain could be a mountain again.

In the moment of Awakening, while my consciousness was landing more fully in the absence of a self, another realization flashed into my consciousness. Everything and everyone is without a me, a separate and distinct self. It was another relaxing exhalation. This understanding of reality was about me and every other sentient being. We each truly had an absence of self as our identity.

The power and magnitude of this realization, this direct experience of true reality, opened to a further realization: everything and everyone is made of pure, connected, unified, unconditioned love and innate goodness. This brought tears of unsurpassed joy, relief, and profound trust in the benevolence of the universe. The universe that was being experienced was kind, loving, and innately good. The universe always had an orientation toward attunement and benevolence for all beings without preference.

Everything and everyone is made of pure, connected, unified, unconditioned love and innate goodness.

In short, the Awakening was a series of realizations that (1) I was not a me, (2) no one was a me, and (3) everything and everyone is an undivided expression of the wholeness of pure unconditioned love and innate goodness. These realizations were my true identity! This was the base reality of all life-forms.

I felt my conceptual foundation shifted in those moments of First Awakening. I was not me anymore. There was a deep knowing that I would never again believe the illusion that we were each a me separate and distinct from every other me, every other life-form. I was free from being anchored to my conceptual me. I was tasting pure freedom.

I knew a deep Awakening had happened. The absence of self coupled with unconditioned, pure love and innate goodness were the new foundation of my Beingness. I was pure love, innate goodness, and pure absence of identity.

Rather than being upsetting or destabilizing at all, it was as though my life was infused with the freshest clean, clear mountain air. I was deeply relaxed in the core of my being. I could breathe the breath of freedom and truth. I was elated with joy. It was the joy of authentic reality. There were tears of relief mixed with indescribable joy as waves of unconditioned love and innate goodness swept over me.

For a few months, I drank deeply from this deep truth of peace, love, goodness, and freedom. I was not plagued by my usual personality workings, with my compulsive behaviors, or with any deficient ache of neediness. I was thoroughly happy, content, fulfilled in everything I did, and at ease trusting the unfolding of life.

1 erroneously concluded this was going to be my permanent inner experience or state. My enthusiasm for this new reality overshadowed my habits of mind. Despite this deep realization, the structures of the self, of the me, were still in place and operating at reduced power. 1 did not know then that the next arduous step would be observing my behavior to identify what was incongruent with this realization and committing to investigate and engage with these discordant actions and behaviors. 1 did not fully grasp then that harmonizing my thoughts, behaviors, and actions with realizations experienced would be an ongoing lifetime endeavor. 1 see now there is no end to realizations nor personal work liberating habits of mind and behavior.

A few months later 1 began to see myself acting in ways that were causing me or others to needlessly suffer. Believing 1 had crossed the finish line of spiritual practice, 1 was dismayed to see that my habitual behaviors were resurfacing.

While our inner foundation can shift in a big First Awakening, it then takes rigorous investigation to uncover what in us is incongruent with the truth revealed in a First Awakening. Sometimes 1 was abiding in and as ultimate truth. At other times 1 was behaving from lifelong habits of mind seemingly stumbling through life. Even when 1 was acting from the life habits of mind, 1 always knew in those moments 1 was acting from a defunct system of identity.

This began the slow process of intentionally bringing my behavior into conformity with the truth revealed. There is more information on this process in the book's chapter on integration and embodiment (see *Pāramīs*/Character Development" starting at page 155).

This First Awakening was later confirmed by several of my teachers. I also had to learn the painful lesson that as magnificent as a new realization is, it typically then highlights whatever behaviors or mind habits are incongruent with that realization. Rather than feeling deflated by this understanding, I now see it as an opportunity to observe my behavior and work to investigate, modify, or change behaviors to be a more harmonious expression of realization. This was my learning that spiritual practice is a stairstepping process. By "stairstepping," I mean that with each new realization, whatever behavior is incongruent with that realization will be highlighted for us to then work on. I will detail how to recognize these habitual incongruities later in this book, starting on page 39, "Daily Spiritual Journal." It will be useful here to explain and explore the foundational pre-Awakening practices and meditations because we need to build a strong, well-secured foundation upon which to reveal the totality of Awakening and deepening realizations, as we return home to the source of all creation.

Foundational Meditations and Practices

In Buddhism most of us start our spiritual path by learning to meditate. The first body of meditations the Shakyamuni Buddha suggested to novices was concentration meditation to begin purifying the mind. Despite there being over forty concentration meditation objects, concentration on the breath was typically the first meditation assigned.

Concentration meditations all encourage you to focus your awareness and attention on the meditative object, prioritizing the object over all else in your perception or awareness, without suppression or rejection. Whatever arises in your awareness that is not the meditative object is not taken up. It is left alone. If, for example, concentration on breath is your meditation, you simply and exclusively focus on your breath. This does not mean we are suppressing or rejecting any mental content or reaction; rather, we are simply prioritizing the meditative object over all else, by choice.

Whichever kind of concentration meditation you practice, you start by focusing on one meditative object to the exclusion of all else, and you begin to witness the functioning of your personality. Your mind shares with you all the things you need to feel comfort and have ease in the meditation.

Your thoughts provide you with ample entertainment to distract you from the breath. Finally, your mind will identify all the things happening that are annoying or frustrating to you and should be eliminated from the room to support your deepening meditation.

From these distractions we will witness all the ways we know our personality and believe in the reality of our sense of a separate self, our customary self-identity. Should we persist in staying with the breath, at an appropriate time our awareness will begin to collect, to unify. It will reveal its natural unified concentration. This unified concentration of awareness as it focuses becomes laserlike in its character. This laserlike quality begins to penetrate our beliefs, our self-identity with our history, and particularly the habit of maintaining a belief in a separate self.

For the reader beginning a meditation practice as part of their journey of spiritual unfolding, I suggest commencing with the concentration practices of breath awareness meditation and innate goodness meditation (both included in this chapter).

Developing our meditative ability in breath awareness meditation and innate goodness meditation builds a very focused awareness that is infused with unconditioned innate goodness. This particular buoyant yet focused awareness allows us to engage in practices that examine, explore, and deconstruct the concepts that make up our sense of self-identity, revealing our true nature or true identity.

Once sufficient stability was reached in each of these practices, the student and teacher would decide which Awakening path was most suitable for the student's temperament and ability. This would mean either deep diving into the innate goodness meditation or commencing a **silent illumination meditation** practice (also included in this chapter) or a combination of both.

Breath Awareness Meditation

Breath awareness meditation is an important foundational meditation that will support all other types and forms of meditation. Including breath awareness meditation at the start of all other meditations will help your concentrated awareness focus and be directed to the meditative object in this present moment.

Breath awareness meditation is called *ānāpānasati.* *Ānāpāna* is translated as breath and *sati* is translated as awareness. Breath awareness meditation is a practice that has the potential and potency to lead us from our simple breathing to the source, the origin, of true reality—*nibbāna.*

Nibbāna is the source of all reality. It is a realm composed of and infused with pure love, pure awareness, and the pure presence of Beingness. It is a love that is profoundly accepting and holds within itself a nonconceptual generative quality that under the right causes and conditions creates life. All life originates in and from the Absolute realm of *nibbāna*.

Breath awareness meditation is quite simple in its instruction: "Breathe, and know you are breathing, right now, in the region between the nostrils and upper lip." Breath awareness meditation helps us to soften and quiet the mind as awareness naturally becomes more focused and we loosen our mental grip on our customary sense of self.

While the most succinct instruction contains all that is needed to undertake this meditation, it is the application of the meditation and the personality distractions that result in this being a practice that takes time and perseverance to master.

Breath Awareness Practice

> Close your eyes. Seating yourself in a comfortable position, place your hands in your lap or high on your thighs. Take a few deep belly breaths inhaling and exhaling as thoroughly as possible. Feel your feet on the ground while noticing the support of the floor in the building you are in. See if you can feel the support of the earth beneath you holding each of us right in this moment.

> Bring your awareness to the region between your nostrils and upper lip.

> Rest your awareness on the breath in the region between your nostrils and upper lip.

> Do not follow the breath into or away from the body.

> Maintain your awareness on the breath to the exclusion of all else. Excluding all other experiences in your awareness means to prioritize the breath over all other sensation, perception, or experience.

> Be with your natural breath.

> As your body and mind settle, your mind will begin to unify, settle, and relax. When you notice your awareness has shifted away from awareness of the breath, gently and kindly return it without criticism or self-judgment.

One way to help support your developing meditative concentration is to count breaths. As a beginning Zen student, I counted breaths for my first two years of meditating. If your awareness wanders easily, it is advisable to count each inhalation and exhalation separately. Once your awareness begins to concentrate and you are staying with the breath more closely without serious interruption, you can start to count each cycle of inhalation and exhalation as one unit. I suggest only counting up from 1 to 8 and then back down from 8 to 1. This numbering helps keep awareness focused. It is important to keep in mind that neither the counting nor the number is the meditation practice. Counting the number of breaths *supports* the meditation. When you can stay with the breath for ten to fifteen minutes without serious interruption, you can try putting down the counting and just be with the breath.

What you will find when commencing breath awareness meditation is how often your awareness is distracted into leaving the meditation. The typical distractions are patterns of thought, future planning and projecting, and replaying past memories of wistfulness and regret.

We must commit to returning to the breath again and again until our awareness settles on the breath in the *ānāpāna* region, between the nostrils and upper lip, and the mysterious depths of reality can begin to emerge.

Innate Goodness Meditation

The other foundational meditation practice supporting Awakening is called innate goodness meditation.

Usually, we receive mirroring of our goodness when we *do* something a parent, caregiver, or teacher praises. It is when we behave the way they wish that we feel seen solely for our doing. This leads us to equate our goodness with what we do rather than with our innate Beingness. Innate goodness is not dependent on any behavior or way of doing. It is an unconditioned heart radiance from the Presence of your Beingness. Innate goodness is a quality of your deeper or true nature. In contacting your innate goodness, you will feel better, more positive, about yourself, feel more at ease, and have greater capacity to be with the *dukkha/* unsatisfactoriness of life. Your innate goodness is the happy, childlike joy we can witness in early pictures of ourselves or others.

Innate goodness is a heart meditation practice that is revolutionary because we are opening to an unconditioned quality of love from our deeper or true nature, inviting it into our awareness, and gently challenging the ongoing inner personality-driven narration of our life.

One of the benefits of innate goodness meditation is its ability to counteract both our negative self-talk and our self-judgments. I do not mean to say self-talk and self-judgments are eliminated entirely; rather, their positionality in our belief system is lessened and reduced when we practice innate goodness meditation.

Innate Goodness Practice

> Close your eyes. Seating yourself in a comfortable position, place your hands in your lap or high on your thighs. Take a few deep belly breaths inhaling and exhaling as thoroughly as possible. Feel your feet on the ground while noticing the support of the floor in the building you are in. See if you can feel the support of the earth beneath you holding each of us right in this moment.

For Visual Meditators

>> Picture yourself or another being in your mind's eye, at a young age when you can easily make contact with your innate goodness.

For Felt-Sense Meditators

>> Remember a time when you were near a baby, young child, or a sweet-natured animal, perhaps a pet. Recall the sweet goodness they radiated. Recall how they did not need to do anything to radiate innate goodness; their

presence alone had a goodness in it. That is
the goodness we are touching into in this
meditation.

> When you are able to be with the picture
in your mind's eye or the felt sense of innate
goodness for ten minutes or more without
serious interruption, rest your awareness
directly in and with innate goodness. Should
your concentration be deep enough, your
awareness will rest comfortably in innate
goodness. If your concentration is not deep
enough yet, innate goodness will begin to
fade from your perception. If innate goodness
begins to fade, return to the visual or felt-sense
memory of one exhibiting innate goodness
and thereby re-establish direct contact with
innate goodness.

Silent Illumination Meditation (Shikintaza)

Silent illumination meditation is a practice that became established in China as Buddhism geographically migrated from India and Nepal to China. Silent illumination meditation is mostly associated with the Chinese **Chan** Buddhist or Japanese Zen Buddhist traditions. It is suitable for both pre- and post-Awakening practitioners.

Effectively, the silent illumination practice involves orienting our awareness to a more unconditioned awareness. In reality these awarenesses are not two. We separate our personal awareness from unconditioned awareness through the application of conceptual convictions. The benefit of silent illumination meditation is that it assists us in softening the concepts of identification, distinction, and separation.

Pre-Awakening, silent illumination meditation supports our slow releasing of concepts of identification, separation, and division. That is, this practice begins to gently challenge our beliefs that we are exclusively a separate self whose life success is entirely dependent for survival upon each of our individual actions. (For post-Awakening silent illumination practice instructions, see pages 141–142.)

Pre-Awakening Silent Illumination Practice

> Close your eyes. Seating yourself in a comfortable position, place your hands in your lap or high on your thighs. Take a few deep belly breaths inhaling and exhaling as thoroughly as possible. Feel your feet on the ground while noticing the support of the floor in the building you are in. See if you can feel the support of the earth beneath you holding each of us right in this moment. You may recognize awareness within your inner perception as having a felt sense like an umbrella, a canopy, or an awning. Be with the felt sense of awareness.

> Allow the concepts of body and mind as separate to soften. Experience the unity of body/ mind as an internal perception or experience of inner flow, moving more freely without the binding of a conceptual separation between body and mind.

> As our firm conceptual convictions soften, we witness the flow of inner and outer moving easily as a unified Oneness.

> We come to realize that it is merely the conceptual separation of inside and outside that keeps us rooted in the belief that outer and inner are different qualities and locations of experience. In truth, inner and outer are an undivided Oneness.

> As our concepts of inside and outside soften, so do our landmarks of here and there, the concepts of beginning and end points or boundaries to our awareness and consciousness. As our conceptual landmarks of here and there soften into a unified Oneness, we experience that leaving and arriving are identical. It is not possible to leave here or arrive there. Everything, including all aspects of direct experience, are always right here, always. The core quality of the universe is hereness, also called thusness or suchness in Buddhism. That means that not only is there no one to get anywhere, there is nowhere other than right here that we can ever abide. These are the

important experiential learnings silent illumination meditation affords us.

> Our connection with awareness in this meditation softens to the point we can feel what should be an end point to awareness yet there is no end point of boundary. Awareness is vast and without any kind of limitation, end point, or boundary.

Daily Spiritual Journal

To have a First Awakening experience is life-altering. Your enduring and closely held views of self and reality become temporarily transparent and are penetrated and perceived as transitory. This perception through our customary self-identity allows us to see clearly the true nature embedded in our consciousness. Our true nature is like a spiritual hologram. When we shine the light of awareness on this particular hologram of knowing, our entire true nature or specific parts of true nature can be highlighted.

This transcendent experience is magnificent. Yet it is not enough to effect lasting, complete change in your life. You are not ready to fully live from the First Awakening experience. In order to begin to live from the changes of First

Awakening, you will need to integrate and embody the new realization, the new view from an activated, functioning no-self.

One of the most useful approaches to integrate your realization is to observe and monitor your behavior. It is the honest self-examination of whether you are walking your talk. I have used, and recommend to students, a spiritual journal to record daily occurrences of incongruence. The incongruences are opportunities to recognize and change our unwholesome behaviors. In Buddhism, unwholesome behaviors are called negative *karma*.

Journaling Practice

Each evening at a quiet time, record in a journal the events of the day that left you feeling uneasy. This would be experiences and interactions where you are left ruminating about your behavior—actions that left you or others feeling uncomfortable.
Here are some steps you can take.

Record a synopsis of each event that day which left you uneasy. Then answer the following questions:

1   Specifically, what action or speech did you use that felt off or flat?

2   What is the earliest memory you have of acting or reacting in a similar circumstance?

3   Who in your life acts this same way, if anyone? Trace back the behavior with the question, Who is this? Are you modeling someone else's behavior or example?

4   Sitting here, with the benefit of hindsight, how would you wish to respond to that same situation again? Replay the scene from that day, changing your behavior, words, or actions to comport with your inner sense of self-identity.

5   How does the new response feel?

Using this method, you will identify historical patterns of behavior. You may see you took on the behavior or reaction of a family member or friend. This practice affords you the opportunity to change your behavior and act more congruently with your inner Awakening. Observing, identifying, and modifying our behavior is the most reliable and repeatable method to institute behavioral change.

There are several important benefits from monitoring and changing your behavior. First, it allows you to act from the Awakening. Altering your behavior fosters Awakening in your awareness. Second, living more fully from Awakening affords you less guilt, remorse, or regret. Third, living from Awakening invites greater inner spaciousness, the canvas for further realizations. A significant benefit of an ongoing spiritual practice is the maturing and developing of our character. It is an opportunity to be more aware, more present, and more attuned to and with our environment and our inner workings.

Here is one personal example. Once when my children were quite young and I was having dinner with them, one accidentally knocked over their full milk glass. The milk quickly ran across the table, into the cracks of the table (where the leaves of the table met) and onto the floor.

Rather than see this as a common childhood accident, I was very upset. I scolded the offender and grumblingly cleaned up the growing pool of milk.

Later, during my reflection time after evening meditation, I recalled a time when I was very young and I spilled my glass of milk. My father reacted strongly, scolding me and lecturing me about growing up during bleak economic times and the sin of wasting food.

I further examined how I could have behaved if I had been acting congruently with my inner truth, rooted in my true nature. In this scenario I explained that being careful and aware at all times was important. And then I simply cleaned up the milk, without reactivity.

Using a daily spiritual journal allows us to maintain an ongoing investigation into our behavior. In this way we can shift our behavior and thinking to be more fully attuned to our inner state of being, which is acting more from our true nature.

Balancing Your Energy: 80/20

Most people, when engaging with another person, project the bulk of their energy and awareness onto the other. This is an effort to feel the other's situation and be helpful and effective. While this behavior is well-motivated, the result of being so determined to fix other people's issues or problems is that we are not present enough to stay attentive to our own experiences or internal process. This is a form of abandoning ourselves and our connection to our true nature.

I had a teacher suggest that I maintain an 80/20 rule. This means that I maintain 80 percent of my awareness on my inner processing and experiences and place, at most, 20 percent of my awareness on the person I am interacting with or other external interactions.

When I first started as a Buddhist teacher in 2007, I had limited public speaking experience. I would get nervous before a public talk. By staying with my direct experience, I came to see that I had about 20 percent of awareness within and roughly 80 percent with the audience, trying to gauge their receptivity and understanding of what I was saying. In real time, I was not only trying to manage my talk in each moment to have it land better with the audience, I was leaving myself to, in some manner, control each member of the audience and their understanding. It did not work. Because I was so focused on the audience, I was losing touch of my own inner experience, the felt sense of what I was conveying, the authenticity of my talk.

Once I shifted the balance of energy to a minimum of 80 percent inside and 20 percent outside, I was able to relax while being in deep contact with the felt sense of the subject matter of my talk. It worked better for me and I received better feedback from my audience.

By maintaining the 80/20 rule, we will be more grounded in our experience and be able to be more authentic in our interactions.

Balancing Your Energy: 80/20 Practice

When you next find yourself alone in a public place such as a large grocery store, department store, or café/restaurant, try the following:

> ›   Find a quiet place to relax and observe both your inner state as well as the world around you.

> ›   Let awareness touch into your inner energy level. How much of your life force energy is within you? How much is outside you tracking and managing the people and world around you?

> ›   Ideally you want to have 80 percent of your life force within you and, at most, 20 percent in contact with the world around you. Try adjusting the balance and see how it feels.

What Else Is Here?

Normally when we experience discomfort, emotional pain, or mental suffering, we presume that the discomfort is the totality of our experience. For example, if I believe my feelings were hurt, typically I would just feel the hurt and conclude that is the entirety of my experience.

In fact, we typically have many levels and lines of experience at any one time. When my students feel a strong emotion such as hurt, I encourage them to ask themselves, "What else is here?" while feeling the hurt place in their body. That is, what else is in their inner experience *in addition* to the hurt feelings?

This is a useful practice to acknowledge that we may have hurt feelings, yet we may also be feeling, joy, curiosity, peacefulness, and/or anger or other experiences. This practice lets us see more fully the totality of our experience in any given moment as well as helping us quantify our hurt and pain as a percentage and location of what we are feeling.

What-Else-is-Here Practice

> In a quiet moment, turn awareness within.

> Make contact with the felt sense of your inner state. What are you feeling and sensing?

> Now, notice where in your body you feel the predominant sensation. For example, you may feel happiness and notice it is located in your head and chest but not in your limbs and lower body.

> Then ask yourself, "What else is here?" This means you sense into the area of your body that is not in touch with happiness. This is to check and see what else might also be present while you are in touch with happiness. Sensing into your limbs and lower body, you might find there is excitement present or maybe smooth- ness or peace. There are endless possibilities for what else may be here.

The benefit of this exercise and practice is to see that we are multidimensional beings. When we experience feelings and emotions, we often take the predominant feeling as the only bodily feeling. That is rarely true. By sensing and contacting the range of sensations and feelings, we can be more landed in our total experience and also learn to touch into more subtle sensations within.

Working with a Teacher

I strongly recommend that each person on a spiritual path of unfolding work with a qualified, realized teacher, particularly when that path contains transcendent experiences.

A realized teacher is teaching from their direct experience rather than from theory or concept. Locate a teacher who resonates with truth in a way you can see. Ask yourself, "Will I be content if I live from a similar realization?" This is important because few teachers can guide students into territories they themselves have not mastered.

A teacher who has traversed the portion of the path you are on can help you meet the challenges and difficulties that can and will arise on an authentic path of liberation. The teacher can validate and confirm what is happening while encouraging you onward.

It is advisable to both attend retreats the teacher offers and work with them one-on-one at least once a month. This deepens the relationship while allowing transmission of the energetic quality on the path where you are engaged. The teacher can then also guide you through the personality and self-identity issues that are certain to arise and toward purification and resolution, supporting deepening transcendent experiences.

Orientation
and
Preparation

～～

IN BUDDHISM ONE CAN ENTER a path of realization through any of the three marks of existence, namely no-self, impermanence, or suffering. I am principally focusing on the field of practices and meditations that reveal the reality of no-self as the portal to Awakening and deepening self-realization. In fact each path contains all of the marks of existence.

The Self in Buddhism and Psychology

We need to understand the self-identity well before we can truly open to transcendence of the self-identity. In this section, we will review the Buddhist perspective of how the self is formed as well as explore self-identity as it is understood in psychology.

Skandhas, *the Building Blocks of the Self-Identity*

In traditional Buddhism, the me—that sense of being a completely separate self—begins with an understanding of the **skandhas** (Sanskrit). The *skandhas* are the aggregates, also called the heaps, that, taken together, construct who we take ourselves to be as a self-identity.

The *skandhas* are form, feeling, perception, impulses, and consciousness.

Form includes all materiality and mentality, including our physical body.

Feeling is usually seen as the reaction to what is perceived. This reaction to our perception is relegated to either pleasant, unpleasant, or neutral (neither pleasant nor unpleasant). The neutral category contains everything we do not feel strongly about.

Perception is both the pure act of perceiving an object and the identifying of what is perceived. For example, if you see a tall branched object in the woods, you might perceive it as "tree."

Impulses are the mental formations containing both imprints of what has been known in the past and any preset conditioning we might have to the object perceived. In our example of the tree, perhaps we remember falling out of a tree when young and being injured and now have a negative reaction to the tree.

Consciousness is often viewed as both the awareness of what we are cognizant of and the intuitive and directly experientially knowing of that same object.

Buddha Nature/Tathāgatagarba

Within each individual's consciousness is a quality of deep presence, of an alive Beingness, as well as an absence, a quality of space that is filled with the possibility of creation without any form or method of identity. This can be referred to as our true nature or **Buddha nature**. Buddha nature means the real possibility that we can open to the realization of Buddhahood. Buddhahood means to be profoundly, if not completely, realized.

In early Buddhism the Buddha was occasionally referred to as Tathāgata, which means "thus-come, thus-gone one." This means that he was present in physical form but had no abiding personal self-identity. His self-identity was in part deep Cessation, profound peace, all-encompassing love, and innate goodness, as well as radiant presence from the Ninth *Jhāna*, the Absolute realm.

The term *tathāgata* means a fully realized consciousness. *Garba* means the potentiality or seed. So *tathāgatagarba* is the seed, the potential, to be a fully realized, fully awake consciousness functioning in the world while appearing as an ordinary person. Within each of us—in fact, within all living beings—is the potential to be so deeply awake that our self-identity is vanquished in the experience of Cessation; Cessation itself replaces the former personal self-identity. One who experiences this shift of self-identity is a *tathāgata*, one who is in the world but truly not of the world. (A presentation of this shift to Cessation as self-identity is in the section on *Daigo-tettei*, starting on page 110, which is the final realization in the Zen Buddhist tradition.)

Another way that the seed of awakeness is represented in Buddhism is by the term "Buddha nature." Buddha nature means the seed or potential in each living being to pursue a path of deepening awakeness with no unconscious motivations.

These terms convey that each of us is already fully realized, awake to the deep mysteries of the universe. Yet this profound awakeness is covered over by unconscious motivations and deep conceptual convictions as to how our world works and who we believe ourselves to be as a separate self-identity. It is through the journey of a consistent spiritual path of meditation, spiritual practices, and personality development that we mature both our spiritual experiences, our self-identity, and our behavior.

> *Within each of us—in fact, within all living beings—is the potential to be so deeply awake that our self-identity is vanquished in the experience of Cessation.*

Sense of Self-Identity from Our Developing Psychology

As infants, we see—or, rather, experience—ourselves and the world as a unified wholeness. There is no separation of self or other, really no me at all except the unified "**dual unity**," as it is referred to in psychology. For more information about this concept, I recommend reading *The Psychological Birth of the Human Infant* by Margaret S. Mahler, Fred Pine, and Anni Bergman.

In dual unity there is a merged perception of Oneness. Caregiver and child, inside and outside, are all seamlessly one. If you have had the opportunity to hold a newborn baby, you might have felt an inclusive oneness of subtle energy. The

55

baby merged by melting into the space your consciousness occupies, including your sense of being a separate me. It can be a heartwarming, tender experience for all.

As deeply touching and tenderly beautiful as the dual unity can be for both caregiver and child, it is not an awake, aware unity of Oneness. It is not a realized Oneness but, rather, a developmental stage of oneness for the baby.

The dual unity begins to erode as the mirrored reality of separateness begins to land in the baby's consciousness. As the baby lies in their crib crying for food, diaper changing, or affection, they begin to understand that what is desired is not within this small, tender body. It is not within the baby's control to attend to their own needs. The needs of the baby can only be met by someone or something outside this little body. The baby learns that sometimes crying and fussing produce results. Other times, cooing and smiling ensure its needs are met with a warm blanket, clean diaper, or food.

The one inescapable fact is the baby does not have the resources to care for and fulfill their many needs and hungers. The impact of this seemingly harsh reality is that the baby learns that they are inside this body that hurts and aches at times, and their relief arrives exclusively from outside, from another. This visceral understanding begins the process of self-identity. The baby is learning that their sense of self, their identity, their me-ness, is from the outer edges of their body inward.

This is the commencing of our identity with the body as a self, a me, separate, discrete, and distinct from all other forms of life. Our bodily felt-sense of me is reinforced by our families and our caregivers, and repeatedly modeled in our societies. Over time, with continued reinforcement we accept this self-definition so deeply that it becomes an unchallengeable fact, a core reality anchored in conceptual conviction and deep belief.

What becomes clear to us at a very early age is that our core life force, our Beingness, is neither recognized nor valued. We find that only when we *do* something valued are we seen and appreciated, even loved. Consequently, our sense of value and our self-identity are structured and dependent upon getting seen and being loved.

Dukkha (Unsatisfactoriness): Our Entry Point on the Spiritual Path

Most of the self-identity, personality patterning issues we struggle with arise due to the *dukkha* of human life. Although *dukkha* is often translated as "suffering," an English word with complex meanings and applications, I prefer "chronic unsatisfactoriness." It covers situations when we get what we want or desire but it ends too early, when we do not get what we want, when we are trying to get away from what we really do not want, or when we are confused about what to want or desire or what to avoid.

The first of the Buddha's Four Noble Truths, *dukkha* is important for the spiritual journey of Awakening and the unfolding of deep realization because it is what drives most of us to commence a spiritual or religious life. To be constantly and consistently beset by a series of life's unsatisfactory events, one after another, can leave us feeling hopeless, helpless, and weak. Out of a spiritual/soul desperation, we search for a spiritual path that fits our temperament and soul orientation. *Dukkha* (unsatisfactoriness) assists us in understanding the fundamental truths of reality while we try to live as an expression of our deepest unborn, uncreated, always present nature.

If you are interested in further reading on this subject, see *Setting the Wheel of Dhamma in Motion: Dhammacakkappavattana Sutta (SN 56:11)*.

The deep truth of reality is that, at our core, our essence, we are not our customary self-identity. A First Awakening in the Buddhist tradition is when the perception and sense of self become transparently clear. It is clear of self-identifying thoughts, memories, and emotional content.

The self-identity is so clear that what is seen in place of the customary self-identity is the source of all creation, which I call the Presence of the Absolute. It could also be called the absence of self.

Absence of Self

The absence of self is an important exploration, investigation, and experience as well as a step toward First Awakening. Absence of self will arise numerous times to allow each of us to gain greater comfort and stability in not exclusively residing in our customary self-identity. We can see, from our own experience, that there is an absence of self, we are unclear exactly who we are, and nothing bad has happened. This gives us greater stability of purpose while soothing any concerns or fears we have about losing ourselves in what is unknown.

Absence of self can begin with a dissatisfactoriness regarding our customary self-identity. The way we self-reference, the mind's insistence on solving any pressing question, and the avoidance of discomfort relating to who and what we take ourselves to be are all signs of the territory of absence of self.

Prior to most Awakening experiences there is a period of time where one experiences an absence of self. This is an absence of any markers, any signs, of who we are. The literal felt sense, when you check inwardly as to who you are, is a complete not-knowing. This is not an idea of not-knowing but a felt sense almost of befuddlement of not being able to discern who you are. Not-knowing can point to an inner sense of knowing where every possible solution to any question exists in this moment. All realization, all confusion, all clarity, all misunderstandings exist in each and every present moment. It is an ongoing inner confusion as to identity. Yet it is an important stage on the path of Awakening. Who and what we take ourselves to be must be questioned to discover what else is present in our consciousness.

The absence of self can be, at a minimum, uncomfortable. The not-knowing can have a destabilizing effect on your inner equilibrium of self. Some people seem to be able to be with the not-knowing for an extended period of time, while others find it too jarring to their personality structures. Everyone seems to modulate the experience of not-knowing. There are times when we are in the shallow end of the pool of not-knowing. Other times our awareness is very much in the deep end of the not-knowing pool. We absolutely do not know who we are and have no idea or clue how to locate a familiar self. It is an expected stage in the unfolding of the path of Awakening.

Some people are not settled enough internally to withstand the deep end of not-knowing. They find old ways and habits of mind to restart the familiar sense of self. They may distract themselves with socialization or media to fully occupy their thoughts. This strategy can drown out the subtle, potent not-knowing present in their awareness. Others seem to have enough stability of awareness and curiosity of heart to sustain the not-knowing. You will not grasp how you will respond to not-knowing until it arises. Should you be someone who is significantly uneasy with not understanding who you are, do not worry if you need to distract yourself for a while. My observation of those who are not fully prepared to inhabit not-knowing as an inner identity is that they distract themselves with customary busy work until the time is ripe to be with inner not-knowing. For the path of Awakening to continue unfolding we each need to be able to stay with the absence of self without judging, fixing, or rejecting the experience.

Absence of self is both a stand-alone experience and a part of the unfolding of First Awakening. It seems that for some people absence of self occurs repeatedly to acquaint them with the experience so there is less resistance to it during the unfolding and flowering of First Awakening.

I have experienced the absence of self many times in my years of meditating and spiritual practice. The first experiences were unsettling and left me anxious and uneasy. I felt the absence of the normal sense of self, yet there was nothing replacing or filling that absence. Part of the purpose of that time of spiritual practice was for me to acclimate to the absence of self. In other words, I learned I could function without a normal self and begin to rest in the quality, the felt sense, of absence. I was increasingly comfortable being no one. In its own way it was liberating and freeing. This increasing comfort with not being me led to a relaxing, a loosening, of the markers of a self. By "markers of a self," I mean the ways we know ourselves. We know ourselves by having a body, having body boundaries and body sensations. We know ourselves by prizing our thoughts and thought process. We participate in our thoughts to the degree that we conclude there is someone thinking. In reality, there are simply thoughts meandering through our awareness.

We also know who we are by repeating our likes and dislikes in a life narrative. This is that inner voice that regularly describes your life. For example, I like that tree, I do not like that car. By continuously and endlessly identifying our likes and dislikes internally, we support and reinforce our sense of a customary self-identity.

As we slowly become increasingly acclimated to having absence of self in place of our customary self-identity, we loosen our grasp on all the markers of self and begin to become comfortable with an inner not-knowing.

In time, I became comfortable abiding without a clear and defined sense of self. I could still know what was needed by this particular body. I could even have clarity about what was appropriate in interacting with others and how to engage thoughts as needed without overly identifying with the thought process.

This acclimation to an absence of self led to later experiences where there was a clarity of perception in the absence of the customary self, which could then open to experiences such as witnessing true nature and being the unity of all is one—in essence, one or more Awakening experiences.

Practices That Highlight and Reveal True Absence of Self

Heart's Yearning

When, as toddlers, we intentionally turn from the unity with the Presence of the Absolute, unity with source, we do so to fully integrate into our family and society. It seems like a matter of our very survival. Yet, in this turn away from the undivided dual unity, we feel a loss, a heart wound, an inner deficiency.

A yearning begins from the pain of turning away from the unifying Presence of the Absolute. It is an ache to be entirely witnessed in our fullness as well as enveloped once again in unconditioned love.

This yearning ache in our heart propels most of us to seek another person to witness and fulfil the ache. Sadly, no personal relationship can fill this deep aching need. As human relationships reveal themselves to be an inadequate substitute for unity with the Presence of the Absolute, we also can begin to blame ourselves by accepting the belief in our unworthiness, leaving us feeling perpetually hopeless, helpless, and lost.

An important part of the journey of Awakening and deepening realization is accepting the deep yearning we have carried for our lifetime. By "accepting," I mean not using distractions to numb or avoid the discomfort of the yearning to return to our true self and true home. This normalizes the heart's yearning and supports our wholesome connection with it.

Heart's Yearning Practice

> Close your eyes. Seating yourself in a comfortable position, place your hands in your lap or high on your thighs. Take a few deep belly breaths inhaling and exhaling as thoroughly as possible. Feel your feet on the ground while noticing the support of the floor in the building you are in. See if you can feel the support of the earth beneath you holding each of us right in this moment.

> Breathe in and out of your heart area.

> See if you can remember instances from your life when you felt connected, whole, in a Oneness with all life.

> Can you feel that connection now? If not, see if you can make contact with the yearning, the heart's calling to be reunited with the Presence of the Absolute.

> Feel the heart's yearning for truth, for peace, for unconditioned love.

> Sense the wholesomeness in aching to return home to the Absolute realm.

When we turn to be with the heart's deep yearning and to be home with the Absolute, we inadvertently stir the superego or inner critic. This requires us to engage with the inner critic or superego in skillful ways.

Working Skillfully with the Superego

The inner critic or superego is a psychological structure that is created from the well-intentioned life admonitions of our caregivers or parents. When we were two to five years old, our caregivers would tell us important life lessons such as "Do not run in the street" or "Do not play with knives." These were excellent life lessons. However, the pressing issue for us as we enter the spiritual path is that we continue to have a superego judging us, criticizing what we do wrong.

The superego's criticism of our actions and behavior develops to a point of being judgmental and condescending. The superego can say things like "That was the stupidest mistake you have ever made," "You are the worst," "How can you be so stupid?" and so on. A large part of the problem with the superego is that we unquestionably believe it. One sign your superego is active is an overall tone of guilt or shame. Recognizing this tone is one way to track the superego from judgment backward to the psychological structure directly.

When cultivating a deep spiritual path, we need inner spaciousness and buoyancy of spirit. The superego, when actively functioning, crowds our inner spaciousness and conveys an oppressive tone of failure. In effect, we feel small and weak when the superego is attacking us. For these reasons we need to learn to work with and defend ourselves against the superego.

There are two approaches when working with the superego. The first is to assertively challenge the aggression of the superego. For people who have experienced mild to moderate life trauma, this seems to be a workable approach.

For others who have unfortunately been subject to more severe or extended life trauma, the best approach is to offer love, almost caring, to convert the superego functions to a gentle ocean mist being reabsorbed into our body.

Superego Practice

For Those with Moderate Life Trauma

» Picture yourself entering the sidewalk gate to a friend's house you are visiting.

» You carefully shut the gate and are halfway to the front porch when a snarling, growling dog appears. You cannot run to either the gate or the front door before the dog would catch you. What do you do?

» Turn and face the dog, pointing your finger for emphasis, and with an assertive voice say, "STOP," "GO AWAY," or "KNOCK IT OFF." You must mean it for the dog to understand your intent.

For Those with Severe Life Trauma

» If you have had more significant traumas in your early life, the assertive approach will embolden the superego and is not recommended for that reason.

» The severe-trauma sufferer needs to meet the superego and its painfully negative,

judgmental statements with love. In doing so,
we soften the superego's anger and aggression
while potentially opening to a reintegration
of the superego into our consciousness.

» An example of loving the superego is when
you feel the harsh, angry pronouncements of
the superego and their crushing effect, or feel
the discomfort, even emotional pain, of the
superego's words and attitudes. As you stay
with the discomfort and emotional pain of the
superego's behaviors, let your heart open.
In this open heart will arise acceptance, compassion, and innate goodness for the suffering
of your superego as well as your own
emotional pain. Thus, innate goodness calms
and quiets the harsh superego behaviors.

» By working directly with the superego, we
are afforded greater inner spaciousness,
wholesome balance, and a greater sense of
well-being. All of these qualities are needed for
the journey of Awakening and the realization
and embodiment of Absolute reality.

» Working with the superego is critical for
a spiritual practice to develop and for our path

> to true reality to open. It is an ongoing
> engagement that we must become skillful
> at to awaken to our true nature.

Purification of Body: Four Elements (Deconstructing the Body as Self)

A substantial portion of our self-identity is rooted in and with our body. The process of Awakening to ultimate reality—to undeniable, unalterable Absolute truth—involves loosening our allegiance to our body as identity.

In this section, we will explore four elements, an ancient Buddhist meditation practice that purifies our conceptual attachments to our body as its own self-identity. A meditative body practice like this one can also assist those of us who hold trauma in our body to contact and potentially release the trauma.

All of materiality, including our bodies, is composed of four elements: earth, water, fire, and wind. We unravel our reliance on form as a component of our identity by under-taking the **four elements meditation** practice. This practice deconstructs concepts by identifying all the characteristics and elements of our materiality, with an embedded expec-tation of revealing what is the core of our sense of self. In effect, we believe that once all the parts of our body are identified, we will confirm that what remains must be me. However, what we find in the culmination of this practice are no abiding markers of a sustained personality. We locate the core, our core, which is an absence of self.

By directly contacting these four elements and their corresponding characteristics in our body, we directly experience how our body and all of reality is comprised of these same four elements. It is comforting to witness all of life as a kind of orchestra playing the same song.

Each of the four elements has at least two characteristics that identify the element through its functioning:

1   Earth: hardness and softness, roughness and smoothness, heaviness and lightness
2   Water: flowing and cohesion
3   Fire: heat and cold
4   Wind: supporting and pushing

When we fully learn and deeply practice the four elements meditation, we can recognize an imbalance in our body, such as experiencing soreness and stiffness in our back and feeling under the soreness to the unimpeded qualities of flowing and heat. This can help to lessen the stiffness we feel in our back and relax more deeply into our meditation. In this way the characteristics of each of the four elements can be used to help with energy blockages or sluggishness in any area of our body.

I personally found this practice to be really helpful. It helped me resolve bodily held traumas. I could, for example, be with my wrist I had damaged or broken in a bad fall when young. I could witness that I continued to hold that wrist as injured or damaged. By bringing the different characteristics of the four elements to the wrist, I experienced smoothness and flow. The practice let me open and witness the movement of energy rather than being with the emotional and historical trauma blockage, the congestion of energy that had been held in place by my emotions about the fall. In effect, this challenges the self-definition as a victim with an injured wrist.

I was able to balance my body and release many of the body traumas held by fear and the emotional contraction against further harm or pain. This proved to be important as my meditation practice deepened and progressed. When a meditation was rooted in another realm of existence, I was able to surrender, allowing consciousness and awareness to journey to the other realm without a great deal of concern or worry about the viability of this body.

Four Elements Practice

This meditation practice uses the same steps to carefully examine each of the four elements and their associated characteristics.

EARTH ELEMENT: *Hardness/Softness, Roughness/Smoothness, Heaviness/Lightness*

We begin this meditation by working though the paired characteristics of the earth element, starting with hardness and softness.

> Start with the breath awareness practice to develop and deepen meditative concentration. (See the instructions on pages 30–31.) When you feel sufficiently concentrated, meaning you are staying with the breath without serious interruption, you can shift your awareness to the four elements' characteristic hardness.

> Slowly scan your body searching for the felt sense of hardness. You will find hardness in your bones, nails, and teeth. The goal is to be with the hardness characteristic beyond conceptual contact. We normally start our meditation using concepts. Meditating on the

concept of hardness would mean using your mind to identify where hardness exists in your body based upon your thought process. Instead, we want to go into the felt sense, the actually meditative-intuitive *contact* with hardness, to directly feel the hardness. You might find while hardness is located with your felt sense, there is almost a unique knowing that arises from identifying hardness aside of its conceptual meaning.

> After being with the felt sense of hardness for ten to fifteen minutes without serious interruption, shift to the felt sense of softness. Every part of your body is either hard or soft. The felt sense of softness will be everyplace in your body that is not a location of hardness.

> When you can stay with the felt sense of softness for fifteen minutes without serious interruption, shift back to hardness. Stay with the felt sense of hardness until you can feel all the locations of hardness in your body at the same time without serious interruption for at least fifteen minutes. It will probably take multiple sessions, if not days, of meditation

before you can be deeply with the felt sense
of hardness without being diverted to other
stimuli.

> Keep alternating between hardness and soft-
ness, each time staying with the characteristic
until you can deeply stay with the felt sense
of hardness and softness for a minimum of
fifteen minutes. Then you can move on to the
characteristics of roughness and smoothness.

> Now move on to the characteristics of
roughness and smoothness and repeat these
meditation steps.

> One easy-to-find location of roughness would
be the bottoms of your feet. Your muscles,
bones, inner liquids are all smooth. Once
you are able to shift between roughness and
smoothness for a minimum of fifteen minutes,
staying deeply with the felt sense of each characteristic, then find the felt sense of hardness
and softness again.

> Deeply contact the felt sense of each of these
four characteristics for a minimum of fifteen
minutes without serious interruption, then

shift your inner focus to heaviness and lightness, again following the above instructions.

> Feel the heaviness of your body as it contacts
the ground. Feel the weight of the bones and
muscles in your body as you relax in a chair
or couch. Relax your muscles and soften your
upright position and posture. How do you feel
and know heaviness? With lightness, make
direct contact with the parts of your body
that are light in weight, light in their quality,
such as liquids and hair. How does lightness
feel to you? Alternate between heaviness and
lightness. Fully feel one before switching to the
other. Know that all of your body, right now, is
either heaviness or lightness.

> Continue with each of these to the depth of
the felt-sense quality. Include all the earth
elements in your meditation, rotating through
each characteristic. Once you are able to
deeply contact the felt sense of each of the
earth element's characteristics for a minimum
of fifteen minutes without serious interruption, shift your inner focus to the water
element.

WATER ELEMENT: *Flowing/Cohesion*

The water element only has two characteristics: flowing and cohesion. Flowing is the movement quality of water. One easy-to-find location of flowing would be our saliva, sweat, and tears.

> Liquids such as blood and water flowing through your body can be discerned with concentrated awareness. Scan your body very slowly to identify and contact the felt sense of flowing. When you are able to identify and stay for a minimum of fifteen minutes with the felt sense of flowing, shift to cohesion.

> Everywhere in your body that is not flowing will be cohesion. Cohesion is the holding together of the liquids in the body. For example, our skin, organs, and veins hold the water qualities of our body. Find the felt sense of all the cohesion in your body. When you are able to stay for a minimum of fifteen minutes with cohesion without serious interruption, shift back to flowing. Keep alternating until you can be with the deep felt-sense of each

characteristic, fully and completely in your body, for a minimum of fifteen minutes.

> Then find the felt sense of the earth element again.

> Once you are able to deeply contact the felt sense of each of these two elements for a minimum of fifteen minutes without serious interruption, shift your inner focus to the fire element and its characteristics, heat and cold.

FIRE ELEMENT: *Heat/Cold*

Heat and cold are temperature qualities of the fire element.

> Sense deeply into your body. Find the places in your body that feel warm to hot. Your exhalation may be a source of heat. Also, your skin temperature would typically be warm. Once you find a source of warmth in your body, slowly scan your entire body to discern and locate all the warmth and heat in it. Once you feel as though you have located all the heat areas of your body, switch to cold areas.

> One easy-to-find location of cold would be our inhalation of breath. The tip of our nose, our fingers, or our toes may feel cold at times. Once you find a cold location in your body, slowly scan your entire body identifying all the places that are cold. When you feel that you have located all the cold places in your body, switch back to the heat areas of the body.

> When you are able to identify and stay for a minimum of fifteen minutes with the felt sense of heat, shift to the cold places in the body and do the same. Keep alternating, then shift to the characteristics of the water element again, followed by the earth element, and finally returning to the fire element.

> Once you are able to deeply contact the felt sense of each of these three elements for a minimum of fifteen minutes without serious interruption, shift your inner focus to the wind element.

WIND ELEMENT: *Supporting/Pushing*

The wind element only has two characteristics: supporting and pushing.

> Sense deeply into your body. As you sit in the meditation posture of uprightness, slowly lean forward. As you return to your typical upright meditation posture, feel the support in your body for holding you and your back upright. This is an example and a direct experience of supporting. Slowly scan your body for all places of support, the places where the body is being held. Once you feel as though you have located all the supporting areas of the body, switch to areas where there is pushing.

> One easy-to-find location of pushing is your belly on the inhalation of breath. You may wish to place one or both of your hands on your belly as you draw a deep breath. Your belly will be pushing against your hands gently resting on your belly. Once you find a pushing location in your body, slowly scan your entire body identifying all the places where pushing

is present. Then switch back to the areas of supporting in the body.

> Keep alternating until you can be with the deep felt-sense of each characteristic fully and completely in your body for fifteen minutes without serious interruption. Then shift to the characteristics of the fire, water, and earth elements as you have done before, for the same duration.

> Once you are able to deeply contact the felt sense of each of these four elements for a minimum of fifteen minutes without serious interruption, cycle through each element. Repeat this process until you can make direct, deep contact with all four elements, fully feeling each and every characteristic in a single minute.

Advanced Four Elements Practice

> On retreat with a teacher who is an expert in the four elements practice, continue cycling until you can complete three full rounds of all four elements, with each characteristic of each element felt individually with the whole of each element. For example, with the element of fire, you would internally say "fire" while fully sensing the characteristics of heat and cold. This is true for all characteristics of all four elements.

> Continue cycling through all four elements at the rate of three cycles per minute.

> When your concentration develops from the first level of concentration meditation, momentary concentration (aware of the meditative object in this moment), to the second level of concentration meditation, access concentration, your body will slowly begin to become clear, a **crystal body**. As you cycle through all of the four elements with

> each characteristic discernible to you, your
> body will become clearer and clearer.
> › During the process of clarifying your body,
> the vantage point of your awareness will
> naturally move to two to three feet above and
> behind your head. Observed from this vantage
> point outside the body, the physicality of
> your body will become more and more clear.
> It will eventually become this crystal clear,
> diamondlike body.
> › Suddenly, at the base of that crystal body you
> will see a heap, a pile of something that looks
> like fireflies. They are blinking on and off in an
> inexplicable randomness.

I remember this practice the first time I undertook it. I had the experiences leading up to witnessing the heap of fireflies blinking on and off. I was called for an interview with my teacher, the Venerable Pa Auk Sayadaw. The Sayadaw smiled as I detailed what was happening. He told me the firefly heap was actually the smallest particles of the physicalness of my body. These are called *kalāpas* in Buddhism. Essentially, what I was seeing were the subatomic particles making up the entire form of my body. The firefly entities were completely real in my perception and experience.

That experience of witnessing myself, my cherished body, as subatomic particles deeply impacted me. Particularly impacted was my conceptual conviction about the solidity of my body. I could never again hold the view, the concept, that I was only this body, this seemingly solid entity. This was experiential proof that my body was not solid. My concept of my body had to shift to include this new reality after witnessing myself as *kalāpas*.

The four elements practice is very useful in helping us to see that the materiality of our body is composed exclusively of the characteristics of the four elements: earth, water, fire, and wind. This is useful in implicitly and directly challenging the unspoken conviction that the true or real me is somehow physically in the body. The four elements practice is undertaken to deconstruct the body concepts we hold as these relate to, and support, our conviction in a separate self, located somewhere in this body.

Lately, I have also been seeing an unknown benefit to the four elements practice. People who have had significant life trauma are finding the four elements practice useful to see the stability of how their consciousness and physicalness is organized. This practice affords to all of us a greater ease being in our body even as we become less identified with the body as a source of self.

As spiritual experiences challenge our conceptual conviction that we are exclusively a separate self, disconnected from all other life, the potential to awaken to an experiential reality of absence of self and undivided wholeness increases.

Awakening

⟋⟍

OUR JOURNEY TO THE DEPTHS of self-realization commences with the experience of First Awakening. Awakening is the direct knowing of the reality of a deeper true nature. This deeper nature, the Presence of the Absolute, lies embedded in each of us from birth. It is quietly, deeply resting as a kind of hologram of spirituality in our consciousness without need or agenda. Should our drive or quest for enlightenment, for thoroughgoing Awakening, not be activated, our deeper nature will stay in a state of repose.

From my perspective, there are three components to an experience of Awakening:

1   A deep experience of absence of self
2   The recognition of one's true nature as one's true identity

3   A thorough unity experience where all is One or everything is a fabric of Oneness

The depth of an Awakening experience is marked by how long it lasts (i.e., minutes versus weeks) and how thoroughly the conviction in the separate me is dislodged short-term as well as permanently.

There are any number of ways that a First Awakening can occur. For example, some First Awakenings occur to people who are on a spiritual path. The path itself seems to be the cause of the Awakening. Dedicated spiritual practices such as prayer and meditation help us orient toward the divine mystery and develop sufficient trust that we can begin to gently question and explore our deepest conceptual convictions about how our personal world operates.

With Awakening, we release our conceptual conviction that we are exclusively a separate individual and temporarily put down our belief that our fundamental flaw, our unlovability, bars us from unity with universal unconditioned love.

I am often asked, "What prevents me from Awakening, from experiencing the ultimate truth in my own experience?" What gets in the way is our firm conceptual conviction that our self and our view of the world are completely separate and distinct. We hold so tightly to the conceptual conviction that I am my usual me that we cannot entertain that we might actually be more, including a not me.

Additionally, there are a number of common inner **resistances** to Awakening. While we may hold the view that Awakening is an important aspiration and goal of a spiritual life, we also have self-preservation fears, anxieties, worries, and terrors that keep us rooted in the customary self-identity hovering just short of Awakening. These resistances to Awakening are explored in greater depth below. As we name, explore, and abide with our worries and anxieties about Awakening, we bring them out of unconsciousness and see them objectively as common human resistances, not foundational defects permanently keeping us from resting in awake consciousness.

There are myriad personal issues held in place by our convictions of the rightness of our beliefs. Until we have the experience, the heart involvement, and some resolution of our fear of death and extinction, we are unable to open to deeper realizations. I view it as a question of ripeness. Just as we cannot ripen green bananas by wishing they were soft and yellow, we cannot force or demand that Awakening dawn in our consciousness. By not getting what we want when we want it, we are developing patience and trust in the natural unfolding of our consciousness.

Just as we cannot ripen green bananas by wishing they were soft and yellow, we cannot force or demand that Awakening dawn in our consciousness.

When we are sufficiently relaxed within and open to all possibilities of experience and reality, our normal sense of self can become more thoroughly transparent; our awareness can perceive the subtle truth of the undivided wholeness of reality that is ever present.

After a First Awakening, in many ways, the real spiritual work begins. We must boldly examine and investigate our life to reveal what is not in harmony with the absence of self, realization of true nature as our true identity, and deeply felt unity experiences of First Awakening. This is why a map of the path of Awakening and deepening self-realization is so important.

Our post-Awakening practice path continues purifying and releasing the conceptual convictions that root our consciousness in the everyday world and its consequent reality. We unplug from our core beliefs about how the world operates. These concepts are replaced by the experience(s) of ultimate reality as our consciousness repeatedly enters into a merging with the source of all, the source of no-source. I use the phrase "source of no-source" to minimize conceptual understanding and rely on direct experience and complete merging with this source. This is why having a realized teacher and a path of practice is vital to deepening realization before and after a First Awakening experience.

In this section, after examining some common resistances, I present the two methods/maps/approaches of Awakening with which I am most familiar: the Zen *kenshō* map and the Theravada **stream entry** map.

Theravada Buddhism is viewed as being the way of the elders. This means that the meditations, teachings, and practices stem from the direct practices and meditations of Shakyamuni Buddha. These are the ancient, traditional practices and meditations closely held and preserved to this day.

In contrast, the Zen tradition developed from the *jhāna* practice of Theravada Buddhism. As I understand it, as the *jhāna* practices emigrated from India to China, pronunciation of *jhāna* changed to *ch'ana*. *Ch'ana* later became *ch'an* in China, and *ch'an* was pronounced *zen* in Japan.

One of the important innovations the Zen tradition introduced to Buddhism was the use of *kōans*. A *kōan* is a spiritual paradoxical problem that cannot be resolved by the use of the ordinary thinking mind. It is an encapsulation of a verbal or nonverbal exchange that results in an Awakening experience. A *kōan* requires us to not only take it deeply into our hearts but also to be the *kōan* to find a resolution.

To give an example, here is one of the most well-known *kōans*, "Mu": A Zen/Chan master was walking with students. They all understood the Zen axiom that all sentient beings have the nature to become awake, what is called our Buddha nature. One student asked the master, "Does a dog have Buddha nature?" The master answered, "*Mu*," which means "no" or "that is absent." The master's answer cannot be true as all sentient beings have Buddha nature. The *kōan* is: What does the word *mu* mean in the context of the exchange between master and student? The student given the *kōan* "Mu" then holds the word *mu* close in their heart. They silently repeat, "*Mu, mu, mu.*" Eventually *mu* is their breath, their very being. The student is *mu*. At some point *mu* may break open the student's consciousness and the nonconceptual solution is known. Typically, the solution is accompanied by a deep *kenshō* experience.

The Zen tradition primarily practices with either *kōan* or silent illumination meditation. Silent illumination meditation evolved from the *jhāna* meditation practices of Theravada Buddhism. These traditions share practice history yet have diverged to find their own expression and philosophical orientation. Zen aims primarily toward Awakening.

The Theravada tradition values Awakening yet focuses more on the meditations and the application of the fruits of the meditations leading to deep realizations of impermanence of everyday life, particularly the experience of Cessation.

Another big difference between the Zen tradition and the Theravada tradition is the end point, the goalless goal of each. In Zen, Awakenings are the focus with the altruistic, self-sacrificing **bodhisattva** (like a saint) delaying their final merging with the source of no-source until all beings are enlightened/awake. In contrast, the Theravada Buddhist ideal is the **arahant**. The *arahant* is guaranteed to be in their final human lifetime/rebirth. At death that consciousness will fully merge with the source of no-source or conclude in an experience of Cessation. That consciousness will never differentiate from the Absolute realm and the enveloping pure love of Cessation again. The *arahant* is not reborn into new lifetimes to draw upon the realizations from prior lifetimes to assist others in crossing over into the land of realization and awakeness. The *arahant*'s lifestream concludes in a final experience of Cessation.

Resistances to a First Awakening

Whenever awareness is gravitating toward absence of self, we begin to encounter our resistances to Awakening or deepening self-realization. The most common resistances are anxiety, worry, and fear or terror.

These resistance patterns typically begin at an early age. They are chosen behaviors that allow us to feel safer than we do without them. While the behaviors may be helpful when initially started, they become automatic programs of reaction and behavior without reflection of the situational appropriateness. We need to see if any or all of these behaviors are still serving us in our present life. Let us look at each resistance in turn.

Anxiety

By "anxiety" I mean a generalized, heightened concern about unknown events. The anxiety may not be specifically related to any one concern or issue. It is more an inner tone of uneasiness and discomfort with the outside world.

Journaling: Anxiety Exercise

Take a few moments to answer the following questions in your journal:

1   What is your lifetime history and experience with anxiety?

2   Are there any anxiety patterns you can identify?

3   When does anxiety customarily arise for you?

4   How is anxiety helpful to you in your present life?

5   How does anxiety lead to *dukkha* (unsatisfactoriness or suffering)?

Worry

Worry is concern and mental preoccupation with anticipated future events. It is tracking and anticipating unwelcome events in the unfolding of life. Worry allows us to anticipate problems and work toward a solution of these problems before they become acute.

Journaling: Worry Exercise

Take a few moments to answer the following questions in your journal:

1   What is your lifetime history and experience with worry?

2   In what circumstances does worry arise?

3   How is worry helpful to you in your present life?

4   How does worry lead to *dukkha* (unsatisfactoriness or suffering)?

Fear

Fear is a gripping concern that we are in near or imminent danger. It is an emotional reaction after we have concluded danger is very near.

In relation to a First Awakening, we can have a host of fears. Some common things we fear about the idea of Awakening include

> dying, extinguishing;
> being lost, endlessly wandering, adrift in an unfamiliar location or space;
> not returning from a deep, unfamiliar space;
> losing our mind or mental faculties;
> losing our identity or fully knowing who we are;
> losing our place in our life and in the world;
> being unable to work or successfully manage life;
> becoming homeless;
> losing control of our mind or behavior;
> losing life activity; and
> losing the pleasures of relationships.

Journaling: Fear Exercise

Take a few moments to answer the following questions in your journal:

1   What is your lifetime history and experience with fear generally as well as the specific fears listed above?

2   Which fear patterns do you identify with?

3   When does fear customarily arise for you?

4   How is fear helpful to you in your present life?

5   How does a fear reaction lead to *dukkha* (unsatisfactoriness or suffering)?

These concerns and fears are called **mara** in Buddhism. *Mara* is the personification of the forces resisting, or opposing, Awakening or enlightenment. *Mara* is the group or category of resistances that arise to stall or prevent Awakening. It can be helpful to simply understand and accept that each of us will have resistances. Which resistances arise will be dependent upon our life patterns of thought and behavior. In other words, we should each expect resistances on our spiritual path of unfolding. They will be the same resistances we utilize and rely upon when meeting challenging interactions in our life.

Working with Resistances Prior to a First Awakening

Our first step when faced with any resistance is to accept its presence. We typically pull back from our resistances trying to both have the safety the resistances appear to provide and resist identifying with the resistance. Within our psychology we both value the resistance and try to avoid identifying ourselves with that particular resistance. Usually each of these resistances do not neatly fit into our self-identity. Acceptance is the first step to acknowledging the resistance. When we can acknowledge a resistance, it allows us to work with it. If we are blind to the resistance in its operation in our life, we cannot objectively investigate its history. Then the resistance cannot be altered or changed.

Our next step in working with resistances is to practice *karuṇā* or compassion meditation and practice. Compassion, as I teach it, is a recognition of our *dukkha* (unsatisfactoriness). Once we recognize it, we need to hold the *dukkha* and let ourselves feel the pain and discomfort that accompany the *dukkha*. Ideally, we want to hold that pain and discomfort in our heart area. When unconditioned compassion arises, it feels like a pair of loving hands helping to hold our discomfort or suffering. Compassion affords us some inner space and tenderness to be with our own *dukkha* or suffering. Compassion does not necessarily fix our issue or problem; rather, it affords us the opportunity to stay with the *dukkha* to witness the unwinding of our *dukkha* or suffering. Then we have the possibility of changing our behavior when employing that particular resistance in life or in spiritual practice.

The next practice step in working with resistances to a First Awakening is the practice of innate goodness meditation. Innate goodness is a quality of our deeper or true nature. It is the unconditioned goodness that is not dependent upon any behavior or way of behaving. (The instructions for the innate goodness meditation can be found on pages 34–35.) Innate goodness meditation counteracts our resistances enough that we can then explore and investigate the resistances with a more objective eye.

It can be useful to identify where the resistance is located in your body. Typically, people will locate the resistance in a particular spot or location in their body. The resistance rarely occupies the entire body. Clarifying where in the body the resistance is experienced helps us to see it is not our entire body. That supports working with the resistance since it appears more manageable. For example, let's say we are experiencing a fear of dying. We check into our inner state and locate the fear of dying from our sternum to our genitals. When we feel clear this is the location of that bodily felt fear, we then employ the what-else-is-here practice (see page 48 for instructions). In effect, we are looking to see what else we are in touch with aside from the fear of dying. We may discover a peacefulness in another location and possibly excitement somewhere else. This practice is very useful to reveal that our fear has not completely overtaken our consciousness. The fact we can witness that the resistance is not overtaking all of our inner state usually lets us feel more at ease with the resistance. This supports our working with the resistance directly.

Finally, our last step in working with resistances to a First Awakening experience is to *gently* confront the fear. This means that we deliberately direct awareness to the resistance as we experience it in the body. We are not doing anything but, rather, simply being with the resistance. We are feeling and sensing its energy. In effect, we are allowing the energy that generally encapsulates our fears and resistances to be felt as fully as is possible. This taps off and reduces the energy and thus some of the physical discomfort associated with that particular resistance. We can then, with the assistance and support of our teacher, explore and understand the resistance and its effects more fully. The more we understand of our history with a resistance, the easier it is to let go of some portion of the resistance in our consciousness.

The Zen Model of Awakening

The Zen model was developed as Buddhism spread to China and later Japan. In the Zen tradition it sees the Zen model as a kind of innovation, a more direct approach, to Awakening.

I spent over twenty years practicing actively in the Zen Buddhist tradition, and I have deep appreciation and gratitude for what I continue to unpack from it. The Zen tradition offers a lot of understanding and framing of First Awakening, particularly with the contribution of the terminology of "no-self," "*kenshō*," and "*satori*." This section looks at each of these terms and what the term is describing in detail.

The Reality of No-Self

No-self is a sustained experience of having no customary sense of self. This is a vacancy of self, but it is distinct from what we call absence of self in that there is a perception of a purity, an openness, a heart quality of deep loving acceptance. Often the no-self experience has broken down the normal inner boundaries and structures that convince us we are separate and distinct from others in nearly every way. It is true that we are completely unique. What is present in the absence of the limitation of self-boundaries is a Oneness, a unity of all life. We feel we are one with everything and everything is a Oneness that contains us. We are included without having to be any particular way. Our behavior is irrelevant to the sustained Oneness. We are accepted, valued, and nourished just as we are. The only judgments about us come from our superego. The pure love of the Absolute realm and Cessation is deeply accepting of every human foible. There is no behavior that will exclude us from the unconditioned love that animates and enlivens all aspects of the universe.

For the no-self to be an Awakening experience it will include, with Oneness, a certainty that all the factors of self we previously used to recognize the self are insubstantial, even transparent. In an Awakening experience there is a deep recognition that our true nature is our true identity, whereas that recognition is missing in a no-self experience. The experience can be an understanding that every self-identity, every personality pattern, that confirmed who we were is fake and insubstantial. Once we see this fakeness and feel its truth deeply, we can never go back to fully believing in the normal self-identity. The customary self-identity may still present itself out of habit and from unconscious triggers in our life.

In some people the experience of no-self will happen many times. The felt sense is that there is not quite the level of comfort or trust to completely release our commitment to our customary self-identity. With sustained contact and experience of no-self, each of us can know the stability and ease of having no set identity. It is an experience of looking in to find a self-reference only to realize that we are looking outwardly. The inward reference becomes an exclusively outward gaze. Rather than being a source of upset, losing the inward viewpoint becomes a comfort, a soothing of our soul, our consciousness. It is soothing in part because we are also in ongoing contact with innate goodness or unconditioned love as a quality of what we are at our core. With repeated and sustained contact, we come to know that our awareness is an undivided part of the whole of the Absolute Awakened Awareness. Succinctly, it is knowing there is no me, knowing I am everything, and everything is a Oneness of love in a reality that is always in this present moment and without hierarchical structure or priority of design.

The term "no-self" is used throughout Buddhism to mean the experience of awareness that does not contact our normal sense of a personality, a me. In my meditation history I have had numerous experiences of absence of self and no-self. Most of these experiences did not fully flower into *kenshō* or *satori*. They were stand-alone experiences of being without the customary self-identity. Sometimes the experiences of absence of self or no-self were destabilizing. They left me uncertain who I was and feeling wobbly inside without the customary self. In hindsight I believe these experiences were conditioning me to gain greater comfort and ease in not having an abiding self. At other times the absence of my usual sense of self was relaxing, a vacation from my usual stresses accompanying a self-identity.

Should no-self open a little further, it can lead to *kenshō*. *Kenshō* is seeing into one's original nature in a direct, usually brief, unquestionable experience of knowing our truth and the truth of all existence in this very moment.

Kenshō: *The Wave Is Sometimes Ocean*

"*Kenshō*" is a Japanese Zen Buddhist term meaning a glimpse into one's true nature. For the majority of individuals who experience their deeper nature, a number of the first experiences will be momentary, flashes of knowing. These flashes of knowing are deeply impactful to an individual consciousness. To see that we are in reality the active, awake, aware Presence of the Absolute and the Absence quality of Cessation is life-altering. Once ultimate reality witnesses itself, it can never go back to not knowing the truth of ultimate reality.

Essentially, *kenshō* is an experience where the self-identity becomes transparent. In *kenshō* we are in direct contact with unity or an undivided aspect of true nature, and we see true nature as our most real, most authentic identity.

If, for example, there is a transparency of self-identity and the experience of throughgoing unity or Oneness of reality, but we do not see our true nature as our true identity, this would not be a *kenshō* or Awakening experience, in my view or teaching. I would call this an experience of absence of self. It is an important precursor experience to Awakening to true identity.

There are varying depths of *kenshō* experience. The depth quality refers to how deeply awareness penetrates true nature and how thoroughly we let go of our allegiance to the ordinary personality as the core self-identity. If it is more like entering the shallow end of a pool, it is a *kenshō* experience, in that true nature is seen, yet we do not see that true nature is our true identity and it is likely we would not be too impacted, affected, or changed by the experience. It is a useful and important taste of true nature, but a shallow *kenshō* typically does not shift our allegiance to our core self-identity.

I talk about the quality of depth of *kenshō* using what I call the 51 percent rule. In my observation of myself and students, until we have a cumulative *kenshō* experience that penetrates to a minimum of 51 percent of our conceptual belief in ourselves as only a separate self-identity, our foundational identity does not change. Should someone have a *kenshō* experience that is less than 51 percent penetration, it would be an important and useful experience. Yet it would neither split open the normal holding of self-identity nor culminate in a dropping of mind and body. They would know on some level they were not just the typical perception of self-identity. Only through a cumulation of repeated *kenshō* experiences or one significant *kenshō* would the sense of self be shattered and true nature become the foundation of identity.

Even when the *kenshō* exceeds 51 percent and the foundation changes, there will nonetheless be a constructing of self-identity following the *kenshō* experience. There will be a foundation of true nature as self-identity while the remaining pieces of the usual self as self-identity try to regroup or restructure. This is where the *investigation* of our behavior to conform to our deepest understanding is a critical ongoing practice. Using a spiritual journal and regular one-on-one work with a qualified teacher aids this developmental process.

Throughout the early years of my meditation practice, I experienced a number of very small *kenshō*. These were instances of a knowing flash where the customary self-identity was transparent and awareness could directly perceive a deeper nature. These were magnificent experiences of quickly touching into true reality. It allowed me to become accustomed to my true nature as a real identity.

If the direct experience of seeing into one's original nature is sustained *and* alters the closely held conviction in being exclusively a separate self, this is referred to as a *satori* experience in Zen.

Satori: *The Ocean Is Each Wave*

"*Satori*" is typically used in the Zen Buddhist tradition to mean either a larger, more thoroughgoing *kenshō* or a series of *kenshō* experiences culminating in a larger, more penetrating Awakening experience. *Kenshō* is a flash of knowing, a toe in the pond of our deeper nature. *Satori*, in contrast, is a sustained dip in the pond including some enjoyable swimming. With the *satori* experience, the foundation of our understanding that we are a separate self independent from all other selves is shattered. It can never be believed again.

In First Awakening there is a visceral understanding, a deep knowing, that our foundation is the Presence of the Absolute coupled with the Absence (emptiness) quality of

Cessation. After a First Awakening experience, our behavior is not predominantly functioning as the inherent wisdom of the Presence of Beingness of the Absolute realm. This takes time with additional, sustained experiences of the Absolute, Cessation, and personal development (i.e., deconstructing the self-identity structures through working with a teacher one-on-one). One difference between the *kenshō* and *satori* experiences of Awakening is that a *satori* experience is more lasting and impactful because 51 percent or more of consciousness opens to the Absolute realm, personified as our true nature.

The First Awakening experience I conveyed earlier in this book (see page 15) was a *satori* experience. It was not only a sustained experience lasting weeks or months; it also forever changed my foundation of self-identity. Rather than the foundation of my Beingness being landed in the customary self-identity, it was now anchored in unconditioned reality of true nature.

Even with this complete shift of the foundation underlying my perception of all reality from self to true nature, I still had the remaining structure of a self-identity operating much of the time. In other words, true nature was trying to express itself. The only identity I was previously accustomed to was my usual self-identity. This led to some beautiful moments of wholesome behavior and actions. It also led to me occasionally acting out of my customary self-identity, injecting a kind of me into my behavior and perspective. Working with a teacher one-on-one allowed me the space and support to unwind the habits of the self-identity and release the conceptual convictions holding the old self-identity in place.

It is not until the Awakening experience of *Daigo-tettei*, the final enlightenment, that the customary self-identity goes completely dormant or ceases. Then the practitioner or teacher is without the old wounds of this lifetime associated with the usual sense of a me. Following *Daigo-tettei*, the practitioner or teacher is rarely triggered by the events and dilemmas of life. After the Awakening of *Daigo-tettei*, there is no me to be triggered. There is no me to defend.

Daigo-Tettei *(Great or Final Awakening)*: *Ocean Is Ocean, Ocean Is Wave,* *and Wave Is Ocean*

"*Daigo-tettei*" is a lesser known or used term in Zen. It is used to convey final Awakening or realization. In the truest sense there is no end to realizations. These will potentially continue as long as we maintain a spiritual path, guided and supported by a realized teacher.

Daigo-tettei is a final realization in that the self-identity, the way we self-reference whenever we turn inward, is thoroughly absent. When we may turn inward to self-reference, we discover spaciousness—a great boundless expanse of deep peacefulness—yet no one, no me, is apparent.

This is not to say that all the life issues of being a human in a world of humans are resolved. From the *Daigo-tettei* realization, we need to once again watch our behavior and reactiveness to see where our psychological structuring, our emotional history, is incongruent with this realization.

From the *Daigo-tettei* realization, we are at a deeper peace, the inner compulsions have quieted, and resting in this very moment (what I call the **eternal now**) is readily at hand.

The experience of realizing *Daigo-tettei* is similar to a *kenshō* experience. There will be a similar experience of absence of self. The absence-of-self experience may be sustained for days or weeks. The *Daigo-tettei* experience will also contain a component of love, of unity, of a thorough Oneness of the entire universe, including us.

One difference between a *kenshō* experience and *Daigo-tettei* is that the *kenshō* experience is usually quick—snap! and it has happened. The *Daigo-tettei* experience is a sloweddown *kenshō* where each component, each psychological or heart shift, is an intuitive choice. We, on some level, accept and open to each shift, each release, each surrender, each turn toward the truth of love, the truth of Cessation.

With first *kenshō* experiences, the sense of self returns within moments, days, or weeks. Only with a sufficient number of deep *kenshō* experiences that cumulate to greater than 51 percent of our sense of self does our true nature land as a foundation of identity—which we call *satori*. Every experience of *kenshō*, *satori*, or *Daigo-tettei* is an immediate experience. The *Daigo-tettei* experience is immediate yet unfolds over a longer time frame than *kenshō* or *satori*.

The transformation in the *Daigo-tettei* self-realization is that the customary self or me drops away permanently. There is a Zen expression that a fallen flower never returns to the tree. This saying reveals that once the usual self-identity is dropped, the source of the universe and all manifestation— what I am calling the source of the Absolute realm or the Ninth *Jhāna*, Cessation—replaces the typical self-identity.

When *Daigo-tettei* emerges, it is usually following the recognition and internal releasing of our deeply cherished concepts supporting the conviction of who we are and how the world reflects our sense of self. We must uncover our core assumptions of identity about ourselves and our relationship to the world. Once these core assumptions, or core convictions, are revealed we need to work with them in specific ways to reveal whether these are ultimately true or not. Whichever of these core convictions we see through as false must be released, allowed to rejoin and merge with source.

Effectively, the realization of *Daigo-tettei* is that every part of who we take ourselves to be is actually rooted in source, not in the personality, its history, and its viewpoints.

When this shift from usual self to *Daigo-tettei*, or self in the Beingness of the Absolute realm, occurs, it is revolutionary. Sensing into our self-identity we find vast, unending spaciousness, the profoundly loving potentiality for manifestation and creation of all life-forms, and an identity that is the identical source of all life-forms.

To return to the model of reality as an ocean and each manifestation of the Absolute realm as a wave of seeming separateness, after *Daigo-tettei* the wave is never known as a separate wave again. The wave always knows it is ocean presenting and manifesting as a particular, unique wave. The wave is an expression of ocean always.

After Daigo-tettei *the wave
is never known as a separate
wave again. . . . The wave is an
expression of ocean always.*

This experience of *Daigo-tettei* is not experienced as a loss or extinction but as pure liberation, pure, boundless freedom. It is the freedom to be wave and ocean simultaneously. Should the wave smooth to still water or return to ocean after crashing majestically on jutting shoreline rocks, it is of no concern to the wave. How can the water of ocean ever leave itself?

I found the experience of *Daigo-tettei* to be simply beyond belief. I had continued with my spiritual practice, extensive retreat practice, and daily meditation since my First Awakening. In those decades I was still, at least some of the time, operating from the habit of the customary self-identity. If a situation in life challenged me, I would often feel the long-suffering, underlying wound be activated. After the *Daigo-tettei* realization, little that life presented landed. Being open and undefended allowed the inadvertent stings and arrows of human interaction to pass through consciousness without a trace, without a ripple.

After *Daigo-tettei*, I knew every viewpoint and perspective had a rightness to it. I knew deep in my bones that every faith of nonharm pointing up the mountain to source was legitimate. All truths were true. In addition, time narrowed to just this present moment. When hearing myself or others speak of the past or future, it was like hearing someone share about a TV program or show they had watched. It was a kind of illusion combined with fantasy. The awareness in my direct experience was always rooted here—in this very moment.

The Awakening Path of Gradual Cultivation and Sudden Illumination

Both before and after any *kenshō* (or *satori* or *Daigo-tettei*) experience is an ongoing practice of cultivation: living our life as wholesomely as possible, attending to our behavior with moment-to-moment awareness, and using our spiritual journal to track incongruities with our spiritual understanding and to trace the superego attacks we sustain. By tracking our reactivity and times when we are emotionally triggered, as well as by defending against superego attacks, we can identify the areas in us that need some attention and work. Keeping a spiritual journal supports our realization by helping us see where we have been changed and recognize where further change is needed as we are acting incongruently with the *kenshō* experience and its impact.

In the history of **Zen Buddhism**, there have been many debates about whether First Awakening is a result, a fruition, of a **gradual cultivation** or of sudden illumination—one or the other but not both. (Sudden illumination is not to be confused with silent illumination. Sudden illumination is the experiential moment of realization.)

Whereas gradual cultivation, as noted above, is the lengthy process of maintaining a consistent meditation or spiritual practice while conforming to a wholesome lifestyle, sudden illumination is the cataclysmic realization, within the unending present moment, that our true identity is true nature—a quality of the functional manifestation of the Presence of the Absolute. We know with unequivocal certainty that we are nothing but true nature undividedly coupled with a unity, a Oneness, that includes every living expression in the world we inhabit.

The following is a Zen story that illuminates the polarizing belief that the single correct understanding of First Awakening is either gradual cultivation or sudden illumination, but not both.

In the history of Zen Buddhism's evolution and journey from China to Japan, there are stories—legends, perhaps—of the mind-to-mind transmission that certified the Awakening of the lead teacher (called a patriarch) for that generation. The Fifth Patriarch Hung-jen, sensing a conclusion to his life and teaching, decided to post a poem and seek replies from those who felt they were awake. Whoever presented a poem expressing the deepest realization would be the next patriarch of Chan/Zen.

There were several senior students who had been spiritually ripening. The heir apparent was Shen-hsiu. In order to communicate his understanding of the gradual cultivation approach, Shen-hsiu wrote a public poem on a monastery wall:

The body is the bodhi tree,
The mind is like a clear mirror.
At all times we must strive to polish it,
And must not let the dust collect.

The Buddha is reported to have seated himself beneath the bodhi tree. He set a firm intention that he would not arise until he was fully awake (i.e., until his then-customary self-identity fell away forever). The bodhi tree is seen by Buddhists as the location of the Buddha's great enlightenment. *Māra* sent every distraction, every fear and temptation to the Buddha during the seven days he remained unmoving under the bodhi tree. On the seventh day the Buddha awoke to the deepest truth of identity: awake consciousness is ever-present and all of life is a Oneness. In this poem the clear mirror represents the foundation of the Absolute realm, and the dust is the concepts of self-identity. The dust must be worked and removed to keep the clear mirror bright and reflecting truth.

In reviewing this poem, we can see there is an implicit belief that there is always dust collecting on the clear mirror of the mind. The dust would be mentalized particles of personal identity slightly obscuring the clear mind mirror. Implicit in Shen-hsiu's understanding was that the dust collecting is not of the same source or substance as the mirror. In other words, the dust is not a manifestation of the Absolute nor a part of the unified field of awakened awareness. It is a matter, then, of continuously attending to the mental activity that yearns to label all experience, creating a concept for direct experience. Thus, it is an ongoing, ceaseless practice to watch for the mind dust to fall on the clear mirror of awareness and, when dust falls, to clean it from the bright mirror.

Hui-neng, an illiterate yet deeply realized student of the fifth patriarch, directed a literate friend to write the following poem in response to Shen-hsiu's:

Bodhi originally has no tree,
The mirror has no stand.
Buddha-nature is always clean and pure,
Where is there room for dust?

Hui-neng was saying that there is no everyday mundane support—no stand—for the mind mirror, this bright realized mind. As our potential to be fully realized, to fully inhabit Buddha nature, is always clean and pure, where can thoughts or beliefs in a separate self-identity even land? According to this perspective, both the mirror or awareness and the mental dust of concept are of the same source. If these are the same source, emanating from the depths of the Absolute realm, why would there need to be any effort to clean what is already pure? This understanding, according to Hui-neng, is right here, always. It was believed that through one experience of sudden illumination all conceptual convictions would be vanquished. (Both poems appear in Philip B. Yampolsky's *The Platform Sutra of the Sixth Patriarch*.)

According to Zen legend, the fifth patriarch confirmed Hui-neng's realization by giving him symbols of his teaching authority, making him the sixth patriarch.

Within the reality of experiential realization, both gradual cultivation, as espoused by Shen-hsiu, and sudden illumination, as demonstrated by Hui-neng, are correct. True Awakening and embodiment of realization occur as sudden illumination and gradual cultivation. Spiritual realization follows an established cycle of expansion and contraction. Realization occurs when our consciousness is expanded in spaciousness beyond its typical limits. As the sudden illumination concludes and we start the process of embodiment, the work of gradual cultivation begins.

When we begin the process of embodiment, we are observing our mind and behavior. In doing so, we witness the places where our inner knowingness of understanding does not match our behavior or thoughts. In effect, we are not fully living from and expressing our realization. This is the expected opportunity to fine-tune our behavior to be more in alignment with our realization. As our thoughts and behavior comport closely with our realization, we once again begin to witness an expansion, a spaciousness occurring within. In the functional reality of realization, both sudden illumination and gradual cultivation are indispensably intertwined.

The Theravada Model of Awakening

The Theravada model of Awakening was presented by the Buddha. It has been the primary, traditional model of Awakening for Buddhists since that time.

In Theravada Buddhism each of the **four stages of Awakening** commence with awareness being drawn and absorbed into the experience of Cessation. Cessation, as I have experienced it, is within the Absolute realm. As our awareness enters the Absolute realm, it is met by pure love and pure presence. It is an amazing, unimaginable field of accepting love with full presence of Beingness. Pure love is a love that does not segregate, that welcomes all and is unconditioned and unborn (it is not born nor does it die). Pure love is not present or responsive as a consequence of any of our behavior. We do not have to do anything or behave in any particular way for the pure love to be fully available.

When awareness is resting in the realm of Absolute, unconditioned reality, it is the full potentiality of all manifestation. In this experience, concept and the perspective of duality are thoroughly quiet. The felt sense is of being undividedly merged into a field of potent awareness. It has an alive viscosity. There are no concepts, no thoughts, no mentality or materiality (physicality) of any kind. Just awareness combined with a deep, penetrating knowing. It is not a personal knowing as there is no location for the perceiving or knowing. It is coemerged knowing without delineation or hint of separation.

Awareness in the Absolute realm is also accurately described as Absence, meaning there are no markers of any self-identity, no bodily sensation or physical awareness, no locus of perception, no materiality or mentality of any kind. Yet it is not an absence that is lacking or missing anything.

Despite there being no movement—no location, even— awareness in the profound Absence seems to drift toward a growing all-encompassing powerful silence. The first few times awareness moves deeper into this absorbing accepting silence, the identity of being embodied quiets; as knowing is quieted, instincts of survival are triggered. It can be compared to a time when you held your breath underwater. The survival instincts were likely activated as you desperately surfaced from underwater with lungs grasping for life, for breath. In moving into Cessation in these first few journeys, mentality desperately scrambles back toward the safety of the conceptual world. Because Cessation is an extinguishing of all markers of self-identity along with all markers of life, it triggers our fear of death. This fear of extinguishing, of death, is a deep and powerful motivation for survival. This survival reaction is to be expected and recognized as a part of the path of Awakening and deepening self-realization.

The impending arrival of complete merging with the Absolute realm, which will be experientially known as Cessation, is appearing in awareness, much like witnessing a solar eclipse. The sun slowly begins to darken as the shadow glides across its surface plunging it into darkness. Suddenly, somewhat unexpectedly, it is thoroughly dark. This is much like witnessing the arrival of Cessation. Our sense of being a physical being silences, our memories and emotions stop, our consciousness and knowing are silenced, and at last awareness itself stops. There is nothing.

With repeated contact and journeying into and through Cessation, our inherent level of trust and joy at returning to source as source overrides our fears of loss of identity as

Cessation fully envelops our awareness, our knowing consciousness itself. In Cessation all sense of being a separate entity is silenced. There is also a halting of all conditioned reality. The Absence of the Absolute realm includes extinguishment of *dukkha* or conditioned unsatisfactoriness, of all conceit of identity or accomplishment, and of all craving including all sensual hungers. There is no craving when deep satisfaction and complete contentment pervade awareness.

The sweeping experience and impact of Cessation can only be recognized after Cessation fades, as perception, consciousness, and awareness return. There is a felt sense of alive, unencumbered freshness.

The sweeping experience and impact of Cessation can only be recognized after Cessation fades, as perception, consciousness, and awareness return. There is a felt sense of alive, unencumbered freshness—a newness of perception, awareness, knowingness, consciousness itself. When conceptual functioning is reactivated, the confident experiential knowing reveals that Cessation was present. Typically, along with the knowing confirmation comes the fruit of this undivided union with Cessation. By "fruit" I mean how awareness and consciousness were altered, changed, or refreshed by complete merging with the unconditioned source of all creation, mentality, and materiality.

One fruit of sustained, repeated merging with Cessation is that the self-identity ceases. It may be replaced with the Absence quality of the Absolute realm. It is the Absence of any conceptual manner of knowing who and what you are. It is direct, filled with every possibility, and made entirely of complete, embracing, welcoming love. In this ceasing of self-identity, absent are the ways you knew you were this person, with these qualities, thoughts, memories, and emotions. The Absolute realm itself fills the vacancy left by our customary self-identity. Our reaction is not a perception of loss or frustration; it is a satisfied whole-body sigh of relief. The Absolute replaces the self-identity. Should there be a turn toward our interiority, rather than landing in the typical sense of self, we find the Absence quality of no-source as what is being referenced. Life then becomes a functioning of all that is unconditioned. The issue of life and death change, too. There is a warmhearted neutrality in knowing the Absence qualities of the Absolute realm will remerge when this particular form of life concludes and is extinguished. In other words, at death this is one possibility where our consciousness will land.

There is potential to have many journeys into the Absolute realm with possible Cessation experiences. Not every journey into the Cessation experience advances one's consciousness onto the next level or stage of Awakening. While you are working on the personal/psychological/emotional/identity issues of stream entry, for example, you may experience several additional journeys into the Cessation experience. Only when the issues are sufficiently resolved, unblocked, and transparent will the next level or stage of Awakening become available as fruition of Cessation experiences. Below, I will reveal each area of realization as well as the ongoing practice highlighted or illuminated as a result of the arising of Cessation.

First Stage of Awakening:
Stream Entry

Stream entry is the first time consciousness has entered and been absorbed into Cessation. Interestingly, the arising of Cessation is not an ending, a removal, a splitting of any identity. Cessation is merging so deeply with pure love and pure presence that all we take ourselves to be—every form and concept of self-identity—is lovingly engulfed in and extinguished by Cessation.

Fully merging in Cessation is an Awakening into the source of all reality, Absolute reality. Part of the impact of this Awakening is a knowing that this is our true identity, the essence of who we really are. As such, the conceptual belief in this separate and distinct personality is shattered. The pieces of self-identity will arise again at this stage of Awakening. Despite self-identity arising again, we no longer believe in a separate existence, a separate self. We know our essential core is none other than the pure love and pure presence of the Absolute realm and the experience of Cessation.

In the stream entry stage of Awakening, the following is true:

> Conviction in a separate self and the view of that self are shattered, gratefully broken beyond repair.

> Any attachment we had to rituals representing the source of all creation—the Absolute realm and experience of Cessation—is also permanently broken. We can see that rituals may *reflect* or honor the source of all love and all presence of the Absence of the Absolute. But elevating the rituals to the same level as reality is released.

> Doubt about the Buddha, his enlightenment, his map of the spiritual journey, or the meditations and practices he elucidated is also vanquished.

Because we are now anchored in the realm of the Absolute and the experience of Cessation, we know with complete conviction that everything the Buddha taught is real, true, and available.

The stream enterer will, post-Cessation, be working on the following self-identity issues:

> envy—coveting of another's possessions
> jealousy—anger at another's receiving what we have wanted
> hypocrisy—acting in conflict to our deepest truth
> fraud—pretending what is not true is true
> denigration—minimizing ourself or another while perceiving from a lack of inherent value
> domination—compulsively ordering others to conform to our personality view

(For more information about this, I recommend reading Nyanaponika Thera's "The Simile of the Cloth, and the Discourse on Effacement.")

In modern Buddhist practice, I am aware of several Theravada Buddhist teachers who became stream enterers by way of a Zen-type First Awakening experience rather than an experience merging into Cessation as is the standard First Awakening within the Theravada model.

Having experienced both, I consider *kenshō* to be equivalent to stream entry. Both see the truth of identity—that our normal personality viewpoint is a conditioned identity, even though self-identity is not ended. Both the Zen practitioner and Theravada practitioner who have one of these experiences have seen through the fakeness of their personality perspective. Yet there has not been sufficient cultivation and investigation of self-identity convictions to uproot the self-identity.

After the first experience of Cessation, and after resolving the issues enumerated above, we may move on to the second stage of Awakening when our consciousness next enters Cessation.

Second Stage of Awakening:
Once-Returner

This stage is called **once-returner** because after this second level of Awakening has been revealed in our restarted consciousness, after Cessation has again concluded, it is known we will have only one more potential lifetime in this human realm. Really what this is pointing to is that our self-identity is weakening in its power and assertions of imposed identity. It will not be too much longer before the self-identity concludes in subsequent experiences of Cessation.

The once-returner is free from the following:

> belief in a separate self-identity
> any attachment to rituals as the source of truth
> skepticism about the practices and meditations elucidated by the Buddha

The following are weakened:

> craving for sensuousness (anything that our senses crave or lust for)
> ill will (wishing negative experiences for anyone)

The main point to understand is that our self-identity-driven compulsiveness and obsessiveness cease. There may still be times when we crave something sensuous or wish someone ill. But these experiences are rare, fleeting, and insubstantial.

The Zen experience of *Daigo-tettei* would probably be here. For the realization of *Daigo-tettei*, the self-identity is extinguished like a candle flame blown out in an expended breath. In the cultivation and investigation stage following the realization of *Daigo-tettei*, there is a keen eye on behavioral missteps—actions and behavior that are not in accord with the *Daigo-tettei* realization. We maintain an investigation to understand the roots of the closely held conceptual convictions as to how the world around us is actually structured. When the conceptual belief supporting the unskillful action or behavior is revealed, it vaporizes like a soap bubble in a heavy wind.

Third Stage of Awakening: Non-Returner

The **non-returner** is not subject to another human rebirth. This means the non-returner would be born in some form of heavenly realm where other non-returners abide and reside. In this non-returner heavenly realm, they would complete the cultivation and realization experiences to be an *arahant*.

The non-returner is free from the following:

> belief in a self
> any attachment to rituals as being the deepest truth
> skepticism about the Buddha, Buddhist teachings or practices, and the community of Buddhist practitioners
> craving of the senses (including all the ways we satisfy our sensual urges or treat ourselves to special delights and pleasures, as well as erotic, sensual lust for another)

> ill will (wishing harm upon another) or aversion (the rejecting of some aspect of reality that we feel is not beneficial or desired by us)

The non-returner is not yet free from the following:

> craving for the form absorption states (form *jhānas*)
> craving for formless absorption states (formless *jhānas*)
> restlessness (a lack of deep contentment and thoroughgoing acceptance of this moment)
> ignorance (if at this stage we were able to release all cravings and restlessness, we would rest in a deep, ongoing, present-moment contentment)

I believe this level of Awakening would also relate to those practitioners who have realized *Daigo-tettei* in the Zen model of Awakening after a suitable period of time where behavior has been observed and discordant actions investigated and liberated from their conceptual source. Once the belief is lifted and the concept thoroughly penetrated by our wisdom eye, the concept fades.

Fourth Stage of Awakening:
Arahant

The *arahant* is fully awake under the Theravada model. It is considered a very rare occurrence. It is believed there are typically no more than a handful of people in each generation who realize the fourth stage of Awakening in the Theravada model. The *arahant* is also not returning to the human realm in any form of rebirth. Effectively, this means the awareness that is the *arahant* remerges with Cessation at the time of bodily death in this lifetime, never to differentiate again.

The *arahant* is free from the following:

> belief in a self

> any attachment to rituals as being the deepest truth

> skeptical doubt about the Buddha, Buddhist teachings and practices, and the community of Buddhist practitioners

> craving of the senses (including all the ways we satisfy our sensual urges or treat ourselves to special delights and pleasures, as well as erotic lust for another)

> ill will (wishing harm upon another) or aversion (the rejecting of some aspect of reality that we feel is not beneficial or desired by us)

> craving for the form absorption states (form
  jhānas)
> craving for formless absorption states (formless
  jhānas)
> conceit of attainments (until this point the
  self-identity will subtly claim all realizations,
  kenshō, or Awakening experiences and convert
  them in part to conceptual holdings)
> restlessness (a lack of deep contentment and
  thoroughgoing acceptance of this moment)
> ignorance (At this stage we are able to release
  our cravings and restlessness. We then rest in a
  deep, ongoing, present-moment contentment.
  In addition, there is no perception of self or other,
  just a unified Oneness of reality.)

Zen and Mahayana Buddhism's Ideal of the Bodhisattva

Zen Buddhism also holds a model of realized living called
the *bodhisattva*.

The *bodhisattva* is one who has realized the deep mysteries of the universe through the once-returner level of the
Theravada map of Awakening. There is an important choice
point after the once-returner level of Awakening. One can

orient toward the non-returner and *arahant* stages and a willingness and commitment to fully merge with the pure love and pure presence of Cessation following bodily death, or one can instead orient toward the *bodhisattva* path, where one is reborn with awakened consciousness intact as the *Vajra* body (diamondlike or luminously indestructible body) to reactivate the Awakenings from prior lifetimes and commit oneself to sharing the meditations and practices and to guiding others to the path of Awakening and deepening self-realization.

The *kenshō*-realized practitioner would be oriented toward the *bodhisattva* model as it is within the Zen and Mahayana Buddhist tradition. The Theravada practitioner wishing to make the vow to save all beings would need to orient toward the *bodhisattva* as a path and forgo the *arahant*'s path.

Processes and Practices
That Support Awakening

Most of the practices in this section—and indeed in this book—are deconstructive practices. Each identifies, processes, and reduces or removes the conceptual beliefs leaving us with a direct experience of our consciousness without conceptual definition or meaning.

They can be seen as practices that highlight the reality of our absence of self, a suspension of our customary belief in the reality of our body and mind as ultimate reality and self-identity. The meditations and practices unravel the cocoon of identity leaving us directly experiencing the reality of our Beingness with no sense of the customary self-identity that is me. This is a gradual process of unwinding and unplugging from our conceptual beliefs. This gradual process of unwinding is what I call the stairstep process.

The Accordion Effect
and the Stairstep Process

There is a phenomenon along the spiritual journey that I call the **accordion effect**. The accordion effect is generally triggered following an expansive openness of spacious awareness in our spiritual practice, usually in meditation.

We have seen expansively from a new vista, for example. Shortly after the new insight, aha moment, or understanding, our personality realizes something unfamiliar has been experienced. It triggers our survival instinct, and our self-identity does its best to collapse in on itself, to protect itself from being extinguished. Our self-identity worries that new experiences of greater openness or expansion can and will result in our death.

It is important to know about and recognize the accordion effect as it will be triggered many times on the journey of unfolding realization. It is simply a part of the process of Awakening, embodying, and deepening realizations. When the accordion effect is triggered, try to remember that it has not collapsed further than when you commenced the new experience or insight. It may feel as though you have taken one step forward and three steps backward. That perspective is not accurate. It is more like three steps forward and one step backward.

I have witnessed in my own spiritual practice, as well as in that of my students, that whenever we have a new insight, aha moment, or understanding, that new understanding will naturally highlight all the parts of us that are not in harmony, or accord, with that new understanding or realization.

We then work on the material highlighted to understand, update, and digest the old unconscious patterns of behavior. Once we have sufficiently understood and resolved the incongruous behavior, we are then open to enter another new expanded, spacious spiritual territory. Once we witness and experience that new spiritual inner territory, that will in turn highlight the personality and psychological material or behaviors that are incongruent with our new insight or understanding. I call this ongoing process of investigation the stairstep process. Should you include this stairstep process in your spiritual practice, the accordion effect will not be as destabilizing or upsetting to you. You will recognize the collapsing action of the accordion effect as a sign you are ready to investigate the personal and psychological issues highlighted by your expanding experiential understanding as part of the process of maturing as a spiritual being.

Silent Illumination Meditation (Shikantaza)

Following a First Awakening there will be a quality of radiance as the *kenshō* experience fades and the Awakening awareness of *kenshō* settles into consciousness. The radiance that we can experience in contacting our true nature can have a felt sense, an energy, of radiant warmth and clarity. It can also reveal a visual radiance of brightness, of luminosity to our inner vision, if we are one of the people with inner vision. Inner vision is not needed for Awakening and self-realization. Some people have inner vision; others have the ability to contact the felt sense, the energy, the direct contact of awareness. Some people have both. Either will suffice for the path of Awakening and self-realization.

The silent illumination meditation (*shikantaza*) practice is particularly appropriate at this stage of Awakening. It is a time when we are in our meditation posture and rest our awareness in and with the inherent radiance, the illumination of awareness. Awareness can be located in our inner state by its felt sense of being a roof, a canopy, an awning over the whole of our inner experiences.

We can supplement silent illumination meditation with innate goodness meditation to contact radiant flowing love in our heart area. With post-Awakening meditation, there is no doing, no goal in silent illumination meditation practice. We are being, not doing. There is no doer to take any action.

Shikantaza is taught primarily in the Zen lineages. It is often translated from the Japanese as "just sitting." I prefer the Chinese-to-English translation "silent illumination" as being more accurate for the practice and fruits of the meditation.

As we begin to see our true nature as our core identity, we will increasingly witness the places in our life where there is a disparity between what we now know as truth and how we typically believe and behave.

What we see and witness as incongruent with our new expanded understanding is our negative *karma*, our unwholesome actions and behaviors. Working with these incongruent behaviors allows us to clarify our understanding while modifying our behavior to be in greater accord with our new realization or expanded sense of awareness.

When we commence silent illumination meditation, we start with awareness revealing the unity inherent in our entire body and mind. The body and mind settle into an undivided Oneness of experienced flow of awareness. The felt sense of the body and mind merging is a quality of inner flow. Inner awareness is not conceptually divided into head and nonhead. The inner flow is body/mind. Yet we conceptually hold our body and mind as separate, two parts. In this meditation, by being with both the body and mind simultaneously without doing anything, the conceptual divisions soften and drop.

As we settle further into silent illumination meditation, perception of inner and outer relax into a Oneness of awareness. The felt sense is that there is a soft distinction between inner and outer worlds. Here, too, the conceptual divide between inner and outer awareness and experience softens into a unified, flowing Oneness with no discernible inside or outside. There is a sense of flowing and cohesion of inner and outer.

After further settling into silent illumination meditation, the Oneness of merged inner and outer awareness expand and extend into a vastness without boundary, border, or limit. Truly, awareness does not actually expand. Our limiting concepts of spaciousness soften and drop through being with awareness, without any intention or doing.

Awareness is a vast, open, inclusive spaciousness of pure perception without qualitative limit or end. Our conceptual definition of body, mind, inner, outer, far, and near soften into a unified field of a profound vast Oneness of experienced awareness.

Post-Awakening Silent Illumination (Shikantaza) Practice

> Seating yourself in a comfortable position, place your hands in your lap or high on your thighs. Take a few deep belly breaths inhaling and exhaling as thoroughly as possible. Feel your feet on the ground while noticing the support of the floor in the building you are in. See if you can feel the support of the earth beneath you holding each of us right in this moment.

> With eyes closed halfway and with a soft gaze, make contact with inner radiance in your heart area. It can be either a visual perception or a felt-sense perception. It does not matter which is present. You may wish to use the innate goodness meditation (explained on pages 34–35) to make contact with the radiance before turning to silent illumination meditation. If you are accustomed to meditating with your eyes closed, you can do the first stage of body

and mind unity with eyes closed. You may recognize awareness within your inner perception as having a felt sense like an umbrella, a canopy, or an awning. Be with the felt sense of awareness.

> Rest with awareness. Just be with awareness. Notice if you sense your body and mind as separate or as one. If separate, there is likely a conceptual block in the neck area. Just be with what is here.

> Once the body and mind flow into union as one, it is recommended to open your eyes ever so slightly to hold both inner and outer perceptions in awareness.

Beingness

In the process of deepening our spiritual unfolding, one of the shifts is from the territory of *doing* to the vastness of *being*. This is a shift from being primarily landed in our sense of self as the core of reality to our deeper, true nature. Our true nature contains the unbounded qualities of the Absolute realm manifesting in awareness and consciousness.

Accessing the many qualities of our true nature puts us in direct touch with the Beingness quality of the Absolute realm, what we can call the Presence of the Absolute. "Beingness quality" means all of reality is emanating from and always in this present moment. The present moment is pure Absolute reality. It is here that all of time is contained. It is here we learn that there really is no doing as there is no one to do. Reality is knowing that all we experience and are is constantly emanating here in the eternal now. All of reality is fresh, new, and flowing always in this very moment. All of reality is contained in Beingness. It may be revealed at some point in our inner unfolding that the past and future are simply concepts. This very present moment is all there is. Due to the quality of flow in the present moment we mistakenly believe there is a past and a future.

Here is a practice for connecting to the unending vastness of this present moment that is the reality of the Absolute realm.

Oneness Practice

> Close your eyes. Seating yourself in a comfortable position, place your hands in your lap or high on your thighs. Take a few deep belly breaths inhaling and exhaling as thoroughly as possible. Feel your feet on the ground while noticing the support of the floor in the building you are in. See if you can feel the support of the earth beneath you holding each of us right in this moment.

> Picture a vast ocean right at sunset where golds, purples, and reds paint the sky. Waves are rolling in unison across the surface of the ocean.

> Imagine you are one of these waves slowly rolling the many miles toward a shoreline. Each wave is unique, perfect just as it is. No wave will ever be identical to your wave.

> Notice how the wave can be aware of itself, its dimensions, fullness, its contact with the water and air.

> Let your awareness drift to the base of you as a wave, where the wave and ocean meet. Are you able to sense or feel the ocean beneath the

> wave? Is the water of the ocean and water
> of the wave the same or different?

> ❯ You can rest in your wave or, if you feel drawn,
> let your awareness move from the water of the
> wave into the water as the ocean.

> ❯ Feel the spaciousness and unending vastness
> of the ocean. Can you feel any edges, any
> limits, to the ocean?

> ❯ Be the ocean, fully inhabiting being water
> in every form or quality. Feel the spacious
> openness without border or limit.

> ❯ After ten to fifteen minutes of being the vast-
> ness of awareness as the ocean, shift to do the
> innate goodness meditation (sees page 34–35).

This ocean metaphor is a direct example of Beingness. Beingness is the aliveness, the depth, the vastness of our awareness. It is not dependent upon anything to exist since it is unconditioned (without birth or death). It simply is as it always has been and always will be.

Within the ocean of Beingness, each living thing appears and is profoundly unique, yet each is of the same core substance or essence. This Beingness is not born and does not die. It adapts much like the ocean when meeting cliffs or protruding rocks; it simply envelops the rock and then recedes to abide in its inherent Oneness.

When we are in direct experiential contact with Beingness, we can feel and have a felt sense of a vastness or a spaciousness, filled with aliveness and calm; Beingness is ever changing to support the arising of life and the quieting of death.

Beingness does not insist on being recognized. It is contentedness expressed in each and every action as well as when resting in inaction.

Another way we can open to and make direct contact with Beingness is through innate goodness meditation. For an overview and instructions, please see pages 32–35.

In practicing innate goodness meditation daily for fifteen minutes, we not only connect with our innate goodness, our innate Beingness, we also make contact with the felt sense, the intuitive perception through contact, of who we are at our core. This is a Beingness that is independent of all labels, all memories, all emotions by which we usually identify ourselves. It is direct contact with our core reality or essence. It is a quality of home, of our true nature.

Eternal Now

In normal society we view time as an undisputed reality of the universe. Because night comes after day, it proves the movement of time for us. Yet time is purely a concept. When we make contact with our own Beingness and begin to abide in Beingness, we slowly discover that a quality of our Beingness is nowness. By "nowness" I mean that all activity occurs right here and right now, always. There is no past or future in Beingness. From the perspective of Beingness, every event that has happened, is happening, or will happen is already happening in this very moment. Every possibility, every permutation of reality, is already present, right now.

The impact of seeing through the concept of time is that we do not look to the future or the past to plan or remember. We can simply rest in Beingness now as we are resting in our most core identity and reality. We are Beingness at our core. Merging and resting in Beingness is a natural, rejuvenating, simplifying experience.

Until we contact, directly experience, and rest in our Beingness, we see our body and the psychological identity of this body as who we are. We strive to receive the recognition and mirroring of others reflecting back to us the reality of identity of this body and the identity in this mind.

One meditation we can engage in to orient our awareness to the present moment is breath awareness meditation.

For an overview of breath awareness meditation and instructions, see pages 28–32.

Thinking Non-Thinking

Our thoughts narrate, identify, and judge our lives while shaping the world we witness and live in. We shift from being a person of customary/consensual reality to being a person of true reality by lessening our unquestioning faith in the conditioned truth of our customary self-identity and our belief in the reality of our concepts and thoughts. Thinking non-thinking is one of the practices in which we can penetrate our allegiance and self-identity with our conceptual holdings and repetitive thoughts. "Non-thinking" refers to the space that exists in our consciousness before a thought arises. This is a subtle territory of our interiority where deep silence contains the impulses to satisfy our direct needs. There is an impulse, for example, of needing water slightly before the thought arises that we need water. We can rest in this pre-thought space and act from the energetic impulses to satisfy our needs when no thoughts are present.

Non-Thinking:
Turning Point Practice

> Close your eyes. Seating yourself in a comfortable position, place your hands in your lap or high on your thighs. Take a few deep belly breaths inhaling and exhaling as thoroughly as possible. Feel your feet on the ground while noticing the support of the floor in the building you are in. See if you can feel the support of the earth beneath you holding each of us right in this moment.

> Draw your awareness to your belly area—specifically, to the area two to three inches below your navel and two to three inches within. In the Zen tradition, this is called the *hara*. It is the seat of spiritual energy and holds our developing and deepening spiritual understanding.

> As you rest your awareness in the *hara*, slowly repeat the phrase "what am I."

> As your meditative concentration develops and deepens, you may wish to shorten the phrase "what am I" to "what." If the shortening of the

phrase is timely, you will find a deepening with the awareness in the *hara*.

> You may feel deeply in contact with the *hara* and not need the supportive phrase. Should you cease using the phrase "what am I" and find awareness is deeply present in the *hara* area, continue belly breaths and being with the "what" quality present in your awareness.

Another meditative practice to initiate contact with Beingness, the source of all manifestation and creation, is to engage the innate goodness meditation with what I call the backward step.

Innate-Goodness-with-a-Backward-Step Practice

> Close your eyes. Seating yourself in a comfortable position, place your hands in your lap or high on your thighs. Take a few deep belly breaths inhaling and exhaling as thoroughly as possible. Feel your feet on the ground while noticing the support of the floor in the building you are in. See if you can feel the support of the earth beneath you holding each of us right in this moment.

> Use your breath to breathe in and out of your heart area.

For Visual Meditators

» Picture yourself or another person or a pet at a time when you can see in your mind's eye your/their inherent, innate goodness.

» Maintain the picture of the individual's innate goodness. Allow it to settle into your heart if that feels natural for you.

For Felt-Sense Meditators

»   Remember a time when you witnessed your or another's innate goodness.

›   Feel and *be with* the energy or felt sense of innate goodness, the connectedness, the freshness, the buoyancy, the warmheartedness of innate goodness.

›   When you feel stable in resting awareness in the presence of innate goodness, you can gently release the mental picture or memory of their innate goodness and directly be with innate goodness itself.

›   Staying with the felt sense of innate goodness, gently expand your awareness in the field of innate goodness. How far away does it extend from where you are seated?

›   What are the qualities of innate goodness you can discern through contact (rather than through thoughts of conceptual understanding)?

›   When you feel deeply present with innate goodness and its field, draw awareness a little

> deeper into the field of innate goodness. Are you able to tell if it is bounded or boundless?
> Are you an observer or is innate goodness observing itself?
> Should the observer be absent from awareness, breathe into the awareness of the field of innate goodness.
> Be innate goodness.

Shifting from observing innate goodness to being merged in the spaciousness field of innate goodness without an observer or even location is taking the backward step. Taking the backward step is being your meditative object rather than simply observing it.

In this section of our journey of Awakening to and realization of our own Beingness, we can also undertake the four elements meditation. See pages 70–81 for an overview and instructions.

Pāramīs/*Character Development*

~~~~~

ONE OF THE METHODS of developing character in the
Buddhist tradition is through the engagement and development of the ***pāramīs*** (*pāramitās* in Sanskrit). The *pāramīs*,
the perfections, are essentially the natural behavior of the
deeply realized. For the rest of us, the *pāramīs* are a guide
to developing wholesome behavior on our ongoing path of
Awakening and functional realization.

These are the *pāramīs*/perfections:

> generosity (*dāna*)

> wholesomeness (*sīla*)

> renunciation (*nekkhamma*)

> wisdom (*paññā*)

> energy (*vīriya*)

> patience (*khanti*)
> truthfulness (*sacca*)
> resolve (*adhiṭṭhāna*)
> loving-kindness (*mettā*)
> equanimity (*upekkhā*)

In order to explore the meaning and practice implications of the *pāramīs*, I want to introduce the Three Pure Precepts. These are simple, direct guides to understand, evaluate, and make wholesome, beneficial behavioral life choices:

1   Do good.
2   Do no harm.
3   Do good for others.

These are direct and uncomplicated. We can hold these pure precepts up as a lens to view proposed action. We are not reflecting on proposed behaviors or actions through the lens of the Three Pure Precepts exclusively for our own benefit. In reviewing whether a proposed action will do good or do harm, we are looking at good or harm to ourselves, to others, and to the world at large. If we use these as a kind of lens to view prospective behavior, we will save ourselves and those around us a lot of suffering.

We are looking to see what the impact of our action and choices will be. The more we engage this perceptual lens on our behavior, the more likely we are to make wholesome choices that will bring us joy while minimizing needless suffering and bringing greater ease to our world.

For example, if we were considering a new job, we could look at it and its activities through the lens of the Three Pure Precepts. If it does good and does not harm others or us, it is quite likely wholesome. It is likely that the pure precepts will orient our choices toward the most positive and beneficial for all beings.

> *If it does good and does not harm others or us, it is quite likely wholesome.*

The *pāramīs*/perfections support greater joy, peacefulness, contentment, and openness. With these *pāramīs*, you will more readily accept deepening contact with awareness, which could result in greater contact with universal unconditioned loving-kindness and equanimity. These heart qualities of your deeper nature support the journey toward deeper truths and open to the Awakening to the truths of the universe.

Understanding more fully the importance of the *pāramīs* for the integration of living the spiritual life supports our orientation and journey toward deeper truths and developing realization.

Generosity (*Dāna*)

When I began to teach in 2007, I did a lot of reading of the Buddha's **suttas**/*sutras*, his sermons. I learned that the Buddha would only teach when *dāna* was present. This had me puzzled. Why would the Buddha only teach in these conditions? It could not be that he, a renunciate monk, was concerned about people's monetary donations. It finally struck me: the Buddha knew that unless a listener was sufficiently in touch with their own heart's natural generosity toward others, they could not be generous toward themselves. The result of being in touch with the heart of generosity was that the listener was more fully open to receive teachings. My learning was that the importance of being generous was not only about giving; it was equally important to be able to fully receive teachings as well as the gifts of spiritual and meditation practice instructions and advice.

Our blocks to being generous generally stem from our sense of scarcity. How much do we worry that there is not enough? Do we have concern that we will never be safe unless we keep accumulating? For most people the roots of generosity and scarcity stem from our birth family and its relationship to money and possessions. If our family, regardless of actual affluence, felt a desperation or hunger toward money, power, or possessions, that craving was likely imprinted upon our consciousness. If, on the other hand, we had open generosity modeled for us, we will be more apt to be open and warmly generous to others and ourselves.

Journaling: Generosity Exercise

Take a few moments to answer the following questions in your journal:

1   When you think of giving money or other possessions to others, those in need, or charities, what arises in you?

2   Do any emotions such as anger, fear, or confusion arise? If so, why?

3   What did you see modeled around *dāna* in your youth?

4   How would you prefer to act with generosity?

Wholesomeness/Virtue (*Sīla*)

Sīla is a foundational support for one's spiritual and meditative practices. Our wholesomeness bears a direct relationship to how, and whether, our meditation practices coalesce and deepen. Wholesomeness is not the only factor in a deepening meditation practice, but it is key.

If we live our life in a way that leaves a wake of harm and upset people behind us, we are likely in some self-confusion about who we are and the effect we have on others. In addition, those who are normally unaware of their negative or harmful effect on others will usually spend an inordinate amount of time in their meditation practice, and on retreat, struggling with restlessness and remorse as they develop deeper awareness of their self-identity and behavior. In effect, they worry about their actions and why their relationships are troubled. These people also seem to have a propensity to imagine what their life would be like if they had made a different decision at a past choice point. They may frequently recall a failed relationship or a career choice that could have altered the trajectory of their life if they had made a different choice. This kind of restlessness and remorse does not solve their angst. We are unable to go back in time and make these different choices and then live out that changed result. It is a form of daydreaming.

In Buddhism we use the Three Pure Precepts along with the standard ten precepts as a guide for our behavior. I have discussed the ten precepts and their meaning in my book *Buddha's Heart*. We have touched on the Three Pure Precepts earlier in this chapter (see page 156). These will be our every-day guides for our work with the *pāramīs*.

Journaling: Wholesomeness Exercise

Take a few moments to answer the following questions in your journal:

1   When you reflect upon your work and your primary relationships through the lens of the Three Pure Precepts, what arises in you?

2   Are your work and personal relationships harming you or others?

3   Do any emotions such as fear or confusion arise? If so, why?

4   Do you feel contentment or satisfaction when reflecting upon your work and primary personal relationships? This can suggest you are living wholesomely in these areas.

5   Are there any changes you need to make?

Renunciation (*Nekkhamma*)

Renunciation is the giving up of something either temporarily or permanently. Typically, we want to employ renunciation to behavior that is not supportive to our life or our spiritual or meditative path. As I grew up in a Christian family, it was common to make a renunciation during Lent. It was a time to put down behaviors in which we were too involved or that had too great a meaning for us. For example, someone who gave up meat might feel they ate too much of it and that they could learn to be more moderate in their consumption. For others, it might be that they liked sweets too much. They wanted to take a break from sugar for their health. Others seemed to make a renunciation over Lent to see if they could stop certain behaviors or lessen their compulsions.

Renunciation is a fairly common tool in working with students. I have had students who made a renunciation of excessive phone usage, internet consumption, fast food, drugs, alcohol, gossip, and even too much planning!

We employ renunciation whenever there is behavior that feels out of balance. Sometimes we can have behaviors in which we feel as though we are losing control. The behavior may be approaching a sense of compulsion. The compulsion feels as though we must do this certain behavior to feel okay about ourselves. We question if we can forgo the behavior. When this is showing up in a student's life, it can be a ripe time to try renunciation.

Journaling: Renunciation Exercise

Take a few moments to answer the following questions in your journal:

1   When you reflect upon your consumption of food, drugs, alcohol, entertainment, internet usage, or social media engagement, do you feel out of balance in any of these areas?

2   Are your consumptions harming you or others?

3   When you reflect upon your consumption levels, do any emotions such as fear, shame, or confusion arise? If so, why?

4   Do you feel contentment or satisfaction when reflecting upon your consumption levels? This can suggest you are living a balanced life in these areas.

5   What would be healthy for you to renounce?

Wisdom (*Paññā*)

One way I describe wisdom is the understanding that comes from seeing nature as it sees itself.

We typically see the world around us, nature, through the lens of our self-identity. In this instance the personality acts as a kind of sonar. Sonar works by a ship sending a radio sound wave outward. When the sound wave meets an object, some portion of the wave is returned to its source, the ship. This returned sound wave provides data that can provide a picture of what is outside of us that we may not be able to see.

Our personality's sonar projects our self-identity into the world. When that self-identity is reflected back to us in an acceptable manner, we feel happily seen and validated for who we take ourselves to be. Should the personality sonar return with a mirroring that we feel does not reflect our self-image of ourselves, we feel unseen, hurt, and rejected.

Wisdom is the ability to have our perception penetrate our narrow self-view and see with an eye that does not need to have a particular response of self-identity. It is a kind of pure sonar that is more of an open question. We do not know what we will receive back from our pure sonar, but it is not being heavily conditioned by our allegiance to our self-identity.

Employing wisdom in our perception includes an openness. There is a willingness to not know what will be reflected back to us. Yet the more we are willing to be open in our perception of the world and of ourselves, the more we will see nature as it is and be in greater contact with the truth that is ever present.

Journaling: Wisdom Exercise

Take a few moments to answer the following questions in your journal:

1   When you reflect upon your contact with the world, how much do you need the mirroring you receive to support your self-identity view?

2   How does it feel to you when you feel another is not seeing you as you wish to be seen?

3   When you are not seen to your satisfaction by another, do any emotions such as fear, shame, or confusion arise? If so, why?

4   Do you feel contentment or satisfaction when reflecting upon your openness to receive mirroring? This can suggest you are living a balanced life in these areas.

Energy (*Vīriya*)

Energy is an important component to a meditative or spiritual life. We need a good amount of energy to both stay with our spiritual practice and deepen our meditation. If our energy is low, we become sluggish and sleepy. When you are sleeping, you are not engaging with spiritual practice or deepening your meditation. Sleepiness is a common affliction for meditators. These days many people are chronically sleep deprived. There are so few true breaks from the demands of our phones and computers that people have little quiet time to rejuvenate energy.

Should our energy be too elevated, we will be agitated and restless. This, too, is a common affliction among meditators. It leaves one feeling fidgety and squirmy on the meditation cushion or chair. When our energy is either too elevated or too low, we are not aware of what is truly happening. We are mentally distracted by the energy imbalance.

In a meditative practice, there is an ongoing balancing of concentration and energy. Concentration in meditation means being aware of the meditative object (such as our breath). If we are engaging in a concentration meditation, we are focusing on the meditative object *to the exclusion of all other sensory data.* This means we turn away from or ignore every other piece of information or stimulus coming into our awareness. If our back hurts, our belly grumbles, or our mind wanders to a conversation we had yesterday, we return our awareness to the meditative object—in this example, our breath.

Should we be practicing another type of meditation, the meditative object can be changing. In mindfulness, we are resting our awareness on whatever is most predominant in our experience. Additionally, we can use noting as a way to be aware of what is predominant without delving too deeply in the content or history of what is most apparent. Noting is a kind of labeling of what is being perceived. For example, we may be experiencing a lot of mind chatter in one particular moment. We can note—or label—this chatter as thoughts.

When energy is too low and we are struggling with a fuzzy-headed sleepiness, we want to recognize our energy is low and increase it. We can increase our energy by getting some rest, participating in brisk exercise, consuming a caffeinated beverage (if we are accustomed to partaking of that type of beverage), or taking in additional light and visual stimuli by opening our eyes wide or engaging in more visual activity.

When we are plagued with elevated energy, we can try to settle down by focusing more intently on our meditative object, adjusting our meditative posture to be upright, or taking a walking break to burn off some energy.

Journaling: Energy Exercise

Take a few moments to answer the following
questions in your journal:

1   When you reflect upon your daily life, are
    you prone to low or elevated energy? What
    strategies do you employ to counteract your
    customary elevated or low energy?

2   Do you identify yourself as an elevated- or
    low-energy person?

3   As you see yourself as an elevated- or low-
    energy person, do any emotions such as fear,
    shame, or confusion arise? If so, why?

4   Do you feel contentment or satisfaction when
    reflecting upon your energy level and the
    strategies you undertake to remedy your
    customary energy level? This can suggest you
    are living a balanced life in these areas.

Patience (*Khanti*)

Patience is one of the *pāramīs* that is desperately needed in today's world. We have never had a world that is as fast paced and time-consuming as it is today. In addition to the fast pace, we are also inundated with ads promoting items we simply cannot live without. This leads to excessive consumption by many of us. The fast pace and excessive consumption are contrary to patience.

Patience is the ability to be very aware and present without expectation of a reward or completion. When I worked as a lawyer, I often focused on concluding the cases I was working, trying to achieve a good outcome for my clients. My actions were undertaken with the goal of conclusion in my mind's eye. Whenever there was a natural delay in a case or a trial schedule, I felt annoyed and impatient. I was impatient because I was focused on the future, not on the present.

"Neuroscience is showing that our minds wander 46.7 percent of the time," says Allan Goldstein, managing director at the University of California, San Diego Center for Mindfulness. My experience working with students is that many people are distracted by the past or the future to an even greater extent. Regardless of the percentages, we naturally resist being right here in the present moment. Our resistance is often based upon our internal discomfort being right here, right now.

As infants and toddlers, we have contact with what we call in Buddhism our deeper or true nature. As we mature and develop our personalities, we intentionally turn away from our contact with our true nature and prioritize contact with the world outside ourselves. What is outside of us feels essential to our survival: our source of food, water, shelter, and human contact. In this turning away from our deeper nature, we feel a loss, an inherent lack. That lack becomes a heart hunger that drives us to spiritual practice. When we touch into this lack, we probably do not remember the time when we felt connected to everything in our world. We felt a part of a wholeness that contained everything we needed or even wanted. As a result of feeling this internal insufficiency, we avoid turning inward to the extent that is possible. This promotes our maintaining an outward orientation while also mentally aligning ourselves with the memories of the past and the possibilities suggested for the future. The end result of feeling this inner lack, coupled with focusing our minds on memories of the past and dreams of the future, means we undervalue what is happening in the present moment.

The power and impact of spiritual and meditative practice happens in the present moment. Orienting to be here, just here, takes patient, sustained persistence. This can be difficult for many people who come to a spiritual practice due to suffering and dissatisfaction. They have a sense that if they can delve more deeply into their interiority, they will find sustainable, sourceless happiness and joy, and they want that happiness and joy right now!

One sign of a maturing spiritual practice is the deep understanding that everything happens in its own time. I recall from my childhood an expression I liked from the Bible, "the fullness of time" (Galatians 4:4–7). In the fullness of time, we understand that we are not in control. Our task is to show up and be as much in the present moment as we are capable of being. We then do our best to deeply let go of any and all results.

Put another way, we learn to be patient for our own ripening. We generally have patience when it comes to waiting for fruit to ripen when we bring it home from the market. We do not typically try to eat fruit or vegetables that are unripe because when we have done this in the past, we have directly experienced unwelcome results. When we wait patiently for natural ripening, we are harmonizing with our own ripeness. Harmonizing with our own development, our own growth, is the functioning and expression of patience.

Journaling: Patience Exercise

Take a few moments to answer the following questions in your journal:

1 When you reflect upon your daily life, what typically takes you out of the present moment?

2 Do you identify more with memories of the past or imaginings/dreams of the future?

3 As you see yourself as orienting toward the past or the future, do any emotions such as fear, shame, or confusion arise? If so, why?

4 How and where does patience show up in your life?

5 Do you feel patience when reflecting upon your progress on a spiritual or meditative path? This can suggest you are living a balanced life in these areas.

Truthfulness (*Sacca*)

To be truthful is to be exactly, precisely, wherever you truly are in this moment.

As children we seek love and various forms of nourishment from our caregivers. To receive our caregivers' pleasure, we learn to tell them what we believe they most want to hear. When we displease our caregivers, we often fear we will lose their support, their love, or our nourishment. Consequently, we learn to shade the truth to minimize our mistakes and errors of judgment to avoid incurring their displeasure. Learning to shade the truth is seen as a survival technique. Few children intend to outright lie. The children simply want the love to continue and to avoid any punishment resulting in a withholding of love.

This skill of shading the truth stays active in our teen and adult years. We transfer our need for approval and love to our romantic partners, friends, and employers. Our drive is to survive while living more in pleasure than in pain.

In walking the path of a spiritual practitioner, we need to be able to be brutally honest and truthful with ourselves and our trusted teachers. It is important to develop the skill to be right where we are with all of our emotional and psychological warts and disfunctions fully on display.

We cultivate an ability to be candidly truthful. Where our attention and awareness are in this very moment is the precise portal into the interiority of our deeper or true nature. Always being right here, right now, is the entryway into our deeper nature. Students often presume that the portal to their deeper nature is only through transcendent experience; while it can be, it can also be accessed from the seemingly mundane work of honestly being ourselves. In either case, truthfulness of the experience of this present moment is what my Zen teachers called "the gateless gate." Being right where you are, right as you are, is the gateless gate to Awakening.

Journaling: Truthfulness Exercise

Take a few moments to answer the following questions in your journal:

1   When you reflect upon your daily life, what typically drives you to try to tell your partner or employer what you believe they want to hear?

2   Is it challenging for you to fully tell the truth? Do you tell yourself the truth?

3   When you do not tell the truth, do any emotions such as fear, shame, or confusion arise? If so, can you tell why?

4   What does it feel like when you tell the truth?

Resolve (*Adhiṭṭhāna*)

Resolve is sometimes equated with determination. In determination there is an embedded drive, a will to make something happen. But I prefer to understand resolve as an inner alignment of intention. In working with students, part of the function of a teacher is supporting their wise intentions.

When we quiet our active mind in meditation and spiritual practice, we can find subtle activity within. Part of this subtle activity within is the call orienting toward returning to our source, what we call the Absolute realm in Buddhism. Feeling the inner call toward the Absolute and the freedom from the pressures of our personality supports our commitment to our own unfolding. This commitment shows up as a desire to find a wise teacher, regularly engage in spiritual and meditative practices, undertake the rigors of retreats where your personal comforts are not primary, and make the life changes dictated by your own unfolding. We can support this growing commitment by setting an intention.

Setting an intention means to specifically and deliberately state your intention to do, or not to do, a specific time-bound action. It is useful to have someone you will report to about your progress, for accountability.

Journaling: Resolve Exercise

Take a few moments to answer the following questions in your journal:

1   What would you like to set an intention to do?

2   What will derail you from accomplishing your intention?

3   When you consider setting an intention, do any emotions such as fear, shame, or confusion arise? If so, why?

4   What would it feel like to successfully complete your intention?

Once you have answered these questions, consider the specifics. For example, if you wish to commence a daily meditation practice, make decisions about the following:

>   How long will you commit to meditating each day?

>   When will you meditate each day?

>   Where will you meditate each day?

>   What meditation will you be doing?

> How long do you wish to commit to a daily meditation (i.e., two weeks, one month)?

> Who will you report your progress to?

Loving-Kindness (*Mettā*)

Mettā (usually translated as loving-kindness) meditation practice is a foundational meditation in the Theravada Buddhist tradition. It is practiced daily by Buddhists around the world. It is regularly practiced because it has profound benefits to the practitioner and those in contact with the practitioner. (You can read more about *mettā* practice in my book *Buddha's Heart*.)

Mettā practice is developing and opening to unconditioned universal love toward ourselves and ultimately all beings. Universal love is the life-force that animates all living beings. It is what causes life to begin for all. Interestingly, for many people the most challenging person for whom to generate *mettā* is *themselves*. Because we have received many negative judgments in our life, a part of us has taken in these judgments and, on some level, believes these to be true. In believing these negative judgments, we truly see ourselves as unworthy of love and *mettā*.

Mettā is simply feeling a warm innate goodness toward ourselves and others. It is seeing the innate goodness in all beings. While it sounds simple in print, it has its challenges. We need to be able to step outside our judgmental beliefs about ourselves and others. This requires us to be willing and able to see these judgments. Some of us have developed the habit of hiding our self-judgments from our view to protect our self-image as a good person. We may hold a belief that good people do not judge others. Yet we accumulate judgments unless we are taught to recognize and challenge the judgments as they arise in our awareness. This usually requires working one-on-one with a wise teacher.

Mettā is a balm for our consciousness. It supports our being in regular contact with our inner warmth, our authentic acceptance of what is happening. *Mettā* supports our experiencing others as whole warmhearted people. We each have a history of unsatisfying love relationships, whether with friends or lovers. *Mettā* untangles our complicated histories with love, kindness, and innate goodness.

Mettā also helps us relax our inner tensions. Some of us know ourselves based upon the various tensions and stress patterns that are a regular part of our life. To move deeper into Awakening experiences, we need to untangle what binds us to our limited view that we are only our personality. We need to be able to know ourselves as an undivided part of the wholeness, the unity of the reality of the Absolute.

Journaling: Loving-Kindness Exercise

Take a few moments to answer the following questions in your journal:

1   What blocks you from contact with your innate goodness?
2   What blocks you from feeling *mettā*?
3   As you feel your blocks to *mettā*, do any emotions such as fear, shame, or confusion arise? If so, why?
4   What would it feel like to have an easy connection with *mettā*?

Equanimity (*Upekkhā*)

Equanimity is a feeling of balance, of everything being in perfect harmony. Equanimity is about accepting the truth of this moment. Any particular moment is created by causes and conditions we can never fully perceive or know. Yet we can accept the moment revealing its truth. Interestingly, this harmony is not dependent upon everything being perfect. It is being with the perfection of nature's imperfections. There is a felt sense of harmonious neutrality when resting in equanimity. (For the practice instructions of equanimity, you may refer to my book *Buddha's Heart.*)

The reason equanimity is a *pāramī* is that when we are internally balanced, accepting, in harmony with all of nature, we are neither resisting nor trying to change reality to match our mental picture or to satisfy our craving.

Ordinarily, we view the world around us as an expression of our inner beliefs and the self-images of our self-identity. In effect, we see the world as an extension of our mental reality. We rely upon our inner view of reality as a shorthand way of feeling safe. If we were in touch with the ever-changing quality of nature and the world, it would mean there is an unpredictability that is outside our control. As humans we derive comfort from predictability.

Equanimity gives us an inner support, a place where we can pivot when faced with life's uncertainties. This place of pivot allows us to be still when there is no movement and to perfectly receive change and return to inner balance and stillness if we are not destabilized by the changes in our life. Having this inner balance and place of pivot supports our journeying deeper into the interiority of our consciousness.

Deeply within our consciousness is the place of contact with universal consciousness. This undivided connection of what seems to be our personal consciousness with the universal, unified consciousness is our reality.

One aspect of an Awakening experience is the witnessing and recognition of the fact our individual consciousness is always united with the Presence of the Absolute. The Presence of the Absolute has qualities of Beingness, hereness, clarity, and awareness. In being rooted in inner equanimity, we can remain unruffled by life and through inherent stillness journey deeper toward the source, the Absolute.

Journaling: Equanimity Exercise

Take a few moments to answer the following questions in your journal:

1   What blocks you from contact with your innate inner balance?

2   What blocks you from feeling harmony?

3   As you feel your blocks to equanimity, do any emotions such as fear, shame, or confusion arise? If so, why?

4   What would it feel like to have an easy connection with equanimity?

Deepening Realizations: Advanced Practices and Meditations

~~~

A FIRST AWAKENING, thoroughly seeing into your true nature as your true identity, is a magnificent event. Our grounding shifts from the customary self-identity to true nature, which is the Absolute realm personified. But a First Awakening is not the end of the path. It is the beginning of the process of bringing our behavior and actions into conformity with our inner knowing. Along with recalibrating our behavior to match our Awakening, we are also moving on the path of Awakening toward deepening self-realizations.

> *A First Awakening is not*
> *the end of the path.*

The deepening self-realizations are realizations of the qualities or characteristics of the Absolute realm. With each successive realization, our contact with the Absolute realm itself deepens and our self-identity with our true nature expands and broadens.

There are a nearly inexhaustible number of deepening realizations after Awakening. These include the formless realms of Buddhism: the Base of Boundless Space, the Base of Boundless Consciousness, the Base of No-thing-ness, and the Base of Neither Perception nor Non-perception. We also have the potential to deeply enter and be coemerged with the Absolute realm and its core, Cessation. In this section, I am offering a practice path for opening to and entering the deepening realizations of a post-Awakening practice. There are several ways or methods to enter into these deepening realizations. I am presenting what I feel is the most accessible portal or entry.

Space/Spaciousness and Concentration Meditation

Space is the first of the formless realms we encounter on the path of Awakening and self-realization. It is usually accessed through the practice of concentration meditation.

Space, functioning as spaciousness, is quite important in the unfolding of Awakening and self-realization.

Vast spaciousness can also be contacted through silent illumination meditation. In that meditation we first settle into a unified body/mind, a personal, directly experienced flow of Oneness. We then settle into a Oneness with what arises internally and externally. These flow in a Oneness in which we are abiding. Then when we settle a little further, a vast, open, boundless spaciousness arises. Everything experienced unfolds in this vastness of awareness.

Through the unfolding of an Awakening experience, our boundaries of body and self-identity soften and relax. As this happens, our inner self-identity is replaced by spaciousness. Spaciousness is who we feel or see ourselves to be when the inner locational boundaries drop away. As spaciousness becomes more of a solid sense of who we are, we begin to be able to journey to realms outside our individual consciousness. We merge with specific realms that are the underlying reality of this universe, of all universes. Space and spaciousness can be accessed through concentration meditation.

Concentration meditation is a process of unifying and purifying the mind. This unification of mind is the felt sense of the concentration meditation deepening. The mind feels to be coalescing, coming together in a unified manner. In the development of concentration meditation, our awareness cycles through three **levels of concentration**: (1) momentary, (2) access, and (3) absorption.

Momentary concentration is when our awareness rests on a meditative object in just this moment. In the next moment our awareness moves to another momentary object. If, for example, we are resting our meditative attention on whatever object is most predominant in our awareness in this moment, that object will change in the next moment or breath. We might be aware of our back pain in this moment only to be caught up in a thought about what we will have for lunch. Because the meditative object is changing, we typically will not move too deeply in the progression of concentration meditation.

Should we continue with a single meditative object, such as our breath or innate goodness, we can deepen our concentration because we are not shifting our awareness to any other object. In this example our concentration could progress from momentary concentration to access concentration. In access concentration we will encounter pleasant feelings and experiences that will assist us in deepening our meditation with greater ease, including the arising of what are called the *jhāna* **factors**.

The *Jhāna* Factors

There are five *jhāna* factors:

1   *Vitakka*—applied awareness
2   *Vicāra*—sustained awareness
3   *Pīti*—joy
4   *Sukha*—bliss
5   *Ekaggatā*—one-pointedness

Vitakka is the action of placing awareness on a single meditative object. In the early stages of concentration meditation, you will need to return awareness many times to the meditative object. As concentration develops and deepens, the process of *vitakka* will be joined by **vicāra**, sustained awareness. *Vitakka* is the only *jhāna* factor where there is any doing, any action that you take. Once the next *jhāna* factor, *vicāra*, arises, the doing will begin to lessen as the practice begins to take on the Beingness of the meditation and slowly replace doingness with relaxed Beingness. In Beingness, the felt sense is that the practice is doing you.

Vicāra is sustained awareness. This arises when, after applying the *jhāna* factor of *vitakka*, awareness begins to maintain its resting posture with the breath. You will see that awareness stays with the breath without serious interruption for five minutes or more. In *vicāra* there is more of a sense of ease and smoothness in meditation. Thoughts are slightly more distant and less captivating. The breath may take on subtle dimensionality and engaging complexity. You may experience a warmhearted feeling toward the breath as the focus and object of your meditation.

Pīti is often translated as joy. *Pīti* really has a range of experience. It will certainly be pleasant and joyous in your experience. Yet it can also touch into rapture. Often when someone hears that a meditation can produce rapture as a natural by-product, they think that sounds exciting. Be aware, though, that intense rapture can involve involuntary body shaking. One of my theories is that the body-shaking quality in the rapture expression of *pīti* has to do with a purification of the energy system in the body. In effect, there are slight blockages slowing the free movement and flow of subtle energy in the body. In the wisdom of the Absolute, *pīti* helps open these blocked channels, allowing for a freer flow of the Presence of the Absolute. This occurs primarily on retreat.

When someone has significant shaking arising, I generally direct them to their bedroom to lie on the bed and invite the shaking. The shaking, as a part of their meditation practice, generally lasts a few days at most.

Sukha is usually translated as "bliss." "Bliss" is a complicated term in English. Culturally we do not use the term "bliss" often in common communications. Bliss is an ecstatic experience of high energy. *Sukha* appears exclusively in the head. It is a bubbly, effervescent feeling of well-being. Everything feels good and there is no sense of any problem. It is a deep easeful feeling in the head.

The fifth *jhāna* factor is **ekaggatā**, one-pointedness. One-pointedness is probably the least known of the *jhāna* factors. Because it is the result, the product, of being meditatively concentrated, it is not an experience most people are familiar with.

Ekaggatā is an important *jhāna* factor. It is important because as one-pointedness arises, it allows our awareness to lock on to the meditative object—in our example, the breath. As this locking on begins to happen, we will concurrently start to relax and release our doing effort. This is the shift from doing to being within the meditation. One phrase that arises for students at this stage of concentration is a clear confirmation that "the practice is doing me." This expression is pointing to the movement from doing to being that is critical in the development of concentration meditation and journeying on the path from First Awakening to full self-realization.

These five *jhāna* factors appear in both access concentration and absorption concentration/*jhāna*. In access concentration, the *jhāna* factors will appear in varying random sequence and intensity. As consciousness continues to unify, the *jhāna* factors appear more frequently with increasing uniformity. Until we achieve what I call high access concentration, the duration and strength of each *jhāna* factor—particularly *pīti*, *sukha*, and *ekaggatā*—will wax and wane. In high access concentration, the *jhāna* factors will present with increasing intensity. In addition, in high access concentration, thoughts become wispier as they cease for increasing periods of time. Body boundaries soften to the point of being barely perceived. The ways you know yourself—through your body, your thoughts, your emotions, and your memories—fade as well. In this fading of identity of body and mind, a felt sense of spaciousness may be discerned. This sense of inner space begins to replace the normal sense of your self-identity. There may be some psychological discomfort as your customary self-identity is temporarily replaced by spaciousness. Resistance to this shift, from customary self-identity to inner spaciousness as temporary self-identity, will slow the deepening progression of the concentration meditation. When the *jhāna* factors are strong and the customary self-identity is permeable and thoughts have effectively stopped, the third level of concentration—absorption concentration—is close. In a miraculous moment, awareness will be drawn into absorption/*jhāna*.

Jhāna is a concentrated state that has a quality of energetic vibration. It has an energy vibration that soothes and purifies awareness and consciousness. It is a state of complete merging with the meditative object in which there is no sense of a me, no thoughts, with all *jhāna* factors present. A first experience of *jhāna* may typically last a moment or two. Over repeated and sustained experience, our consciousness will be able to stay merged with First *Jhāna* for minutes, even hours. Each moment we stay merged in First *Jhāna* is a moment of purification of mind and lessening of negative karma.

There are four form *jhānas*. Each form *jhāna* feels to be within the reach of consciousness in this body. That is, it feels to be contained in the form of our consciousness. The practice of the four form *jhānas* is described in the book I coauthored called *Practicing the Jhānas*.

In contrast the four formless *jhānas* feel to be realms outside of our body. The felt sense in merging into a formless realm is that our consciousness travels through the top of our head, sometimes referred to as the crown chakra, to a particular formless realm.

Formless Realms/
Formless *Jhānas*

In Theravada Buddhism there are four formless realms called the four formless *jhānas*. The formless realms are nondual. By "nondual," I mean there is neither perception nor awareness of a particularized me or anything we could identify as not me. Abiding in these realms is a direct, merged awareness with the particular quality of that realm. Each realm, as we move closer to the Absolute realm, is simpler yet further refined in breathtaking delicacy than the prior realm.

> *Each realm, as we move closer to the Absolute realm, is simpler yet further refined in breathtaking delicacy than the prior realm.*

The formless realms are an important part of the path from First Awakening to full self-realization. They are important because each is a quality, a dimension, of the Absolute realm. The Absolute realm is the source of all creation and in its center is the potential for the experience of

Cessation. Consider Cessation as the quality of the universe before any life, or Beingness, existed. Cessation is experienced as a primordial, dark, soundless silence devoid of all conceptual knowing, filled with thoroughly accepting pure love. The dark recesses of Cessation are the source of light, sound, and movement. As you realize the formless realms and continue immersing in them, the merging of individual consciousness and the Absolute consciousness as expressed by the particular formless realm are revealed as an undivided Oneness.

With each realm we can experience these from a subjective or objective perspective. The benefit of such an experience is opening our consciousness to experientially know awareness can be in one particular location or everywhere. In a subjective experience, we feel there is a location of awareness, a place from which awareness is perceiving. In contrast, in the objective experience there is not one location of awareness. Awareness is everywhere in the vastness of that realm. Perception arises from everywhere in the objective experience of perception and awareness.

These are the four formless realms/*jhānas*:

> the Base of Boundless Space (the Fifth *Jhāna*)
> the Base of Boundless Consciousness (the Sixth *Jhāna*)

> the Base of Boundless No-thing-ness (the Seventh *Jhāna*)

> the Base of Neither Perception nor Non-perception (the Eighth *Jhāna*)

I have found that, for myself and a few students, the formless realms can experientially open in consciousness without always requiring the deep focus of absorption in concentration meditation. When the Absolute realm is functioning in our consciousness and awareness, it is possible for any or all of the formless realms to appear and open.

The Fifth Jhāna:
The Base of Boundless Space

The Base of Boundless Space, as its name suggests, is the quality of the Absolute realm that is expressed and reflected by unending, infinite space. Its infinite nature confirms that the Absolute realm has no conditioning, boundaries, or limits. The quality of space can extend everywhere and nowhere. The fact that space extends nowhere means that every form of materiality, of reality itself, is contained in this very moment in space, always. Space exists in the smallest subatomic particle. The fact that every material form of reality contains space means that nothing is truly solid or unchanging in the material world, including us. We are not so solid or fixed that we are incapable of change.

The fact that we are capable of constant unending change aligns our understanding of reality with the fluid, adaptable aspect of the Absolute realm. The quality of fluidity confirms that everything we view as reality—from the world around us to our personality—are capable of movement and change at any time. Because we are not fixed in time or place due to the fluidity and flow of the spacious quality of the Absolute realm, we are allowed to be in the eternal nowness of the Absolute realm. The eternal now is the true representation of time and location. There is only right here and always right now. This is always true.

I spent two months on a dedicated *samatha* meditation retreat nearly twenty years ago. During that retreat I worked with and attained all nine *jhānas* to the level of mastery. *Jhāna* mastery takes very deep concentration and an ability to release any sense of a me for long periods of time.

My experience with the Base of Boundless Space was of being in a realm predominantly containing unending vastness. This experience helped the limiting concepts of location and perspective soften and, on occasion, drop. When these concepts were dropped, even temporarily, it was liberating. What I took to be my consciousness was inseparable from expansive, unbounded awareness. This experience of expansiveness commenced with entry into the Base of Boundless Space.

Boundless Space Practice

There are a number of practices or meditations that can open awareness to the vast, unbounded quality of boundless space. Here I present one approach using silent illumination meditation.

> Seating yourself in a comfortable position, place your hands in your lap or high on your thighs. Take a few deep belly breaths inhaling and exhaling as thoroughly as possible. Feel your feet on the ground while noticing the support of the floor in the building you are in. See if you can feel the support of the earth beneath you holding each of us right in this moment.

> Rest with awareness. Just be with awareness. Notice if you sense your body and mind as separate or as one. If separate, there is likely a conceptual block in the neck area. Just be with what is here.

> As this practice deepens through steeping in stillness of awareness, it first unifies body and

mind. We experience a perception of Oneness of body and mind. Whether we experience a thought or a physical sensation, it is always experienced in this unified Oneness of body/mind.

> In deepening still further in the unified body/mind, we find a unity, a Oneness of inside and outside. There is no separation of inner or outer content of experience. All activity is expressed from this unified Oneness of inside/outside.

> When our contact and meditative concentration deepens further, the felt unity of body/mind and inside/outside expands in a field of vastness. This is a vastness of unbounded space. The vastness of this felt-sense space becomes our meditative object.

> Your awareness and the vast space containing all awareness are one. This unity of awareness and vast spaciousness holding all of awareness is our sole focus.

> Steep in this unified field of awareness and the space holding or containing awareness for at least an hour without serious interruption.

> As the vastness becomes landed in our con-
> sciousness through direct experience, we are
> drawn to know the consciousness that holds or
> contains vast, unending space. Our awareness
> can then be drawn into the universal con-
> sciousness that holds the vastness of unending
> space in the Base of Boundless Space realm.

The Sixth Jhāna:
The Base of Boundless Consciousness

The Base of Boundless Consciousness is an important realm
to experience. Steeping in boundless consciousness supports our deep understanding, our deep knowing, that our
individual, localized consciousness is not fixed or limited by
our body or mind.

We normally view our consciousness—our knowing
awareness—as being located in this particular body and
mind. We do not experience it as being anywhere else.
Because we view our consciousness as being fixed and contained near our body, we are not usually aware that it is a
seemingly segregated portion of the boundless consciousness of the Absolute realm. Consequently, we view ourselves
as limited by our body and mind. We cannot easily see or

know that we are an expression of an undivided wholeness of consciousness of the Absolute realm.

In reality, our individual, localized consciousness is always in an undivided, merged wholeness with the Absolute realm, the Absolute consciousness. With sustained abiding in the Base of Boundless Consciousness, we can experience the endless, infinite, coemerged consciousness of which we are a part and a particular, unique expression.

One of the principal differences between the Base of Boundless Space and the Base of Boundless Consciousness is the knowing quality in the Base of Boundless Consciousness. In boundless space there is an implicit knowing of vastness and being unbounded by any concept of limitation. With boundless consciousness, we also are in direct contact with a knowing that all form and formless realities originate in and from the same source. We see that all of the world of form, including our everyday world, is coming from formlessness into form and then, at the appropriate time, returning to their source of formlessness—just as all of form eventually dissolves into smaller pieces that eventually return to sub-atomic particles, what we call *kalāpas* in Buddhism.

Boundless Consciousness Practice

There are a number of practices or meditations that can open awareness to the vast, unbounded quality of boundless consciousness. Here I present one approach using silent illumination meditation.

> Reestablish your silent illumination meditation practice (described on pages 141–142).

> Continue with the meditation as your body/mind merge, inside/outside merge, and awareness opens to a vast, unbounded spaciousness. Rest in the merged field of awareness and the space holding vast awareness for an hour or more without serious interruption.

> Allow your awareness to shift slightly to the consciousness holding vast, unbounded space. It is vast, unbounded consciousness.

> Allow awareness to merge with vast, unbounded consciousness. Rest in the field of awareness merged with the unbounded

> consciousness containing vast, unbounded
> space for an hour or more without serious
> interruption. You may recognize awareness
> within your inner perception as having a felt
> sense like an umbrella, a canopy, or an awning.
> Be with the felt sense of awareness.

We will now turn our meditative focus to the vast, unbounded no-thing-ness that holds vast, unbounded consciousness.

The Seventh Jhāna*:*
The Base of Boundless No-thing-ness

The Base of Boundless No-thing-ness is an important realization to experience. The no-thing-ness quality of the Absolute realm is absent of any expression or form of what is manifest. It is an absence of movement, of living reality. It is the quiet, dark, infinite stillness that is ever-present in life.

Every expression of life, color, or movement in the world contains stillness, contains no-thing-ness. In fact, there cannot be movement, activity, or shape to our world without there also being no-thing-ness present. We cannot have a something unless we simultaneously have a nothing.

In addition, as part of our path to full self-realization we need to have our awake awareness be steeped in no-thing-ness. We need to be at ease without any movement, sound, or shape. In part this is providing us with experiential understanding of all aspects of the Absolute realm. It is also a preparation for us to approach the experience of Cessation when abiding in and as the absence quality of the Absolute realm.

Steeping in no-thing-ness also allows our consciousness to know primordial nothing from which everything arises or manifests. Much of our everyday motivations to do various activities are to fill silence, to fill space, to fill nothing with any kind of something. This nothing stirs our deep-seated concerns and fears about death and extinction. By steeping our consciousness in the realm of no-thing-ness, we reveal these deep fears and realign our concerns with the reality of no-thing-ness. By steeping in no-thing-ness, we come to the realization that no-thing-ness is not only who we are as an identity but also who we are in our physicality. By this, I mean that our physicialness is also an expression of no-thing-ness. This is deeply realizing the line from the *Heart Sutra* that "form is emptiness, emptiness is form." This line is not saying form becomes emptiness (or absence) but, rather, that form *is* emptiness. These are codependent and mutually arising.

Boundless No-thing-ness Practice

There are a number of practices or meditations that can open awareness to the vast, unbounded quality of boundless no-thing-ness. Here I present one approach using silent illumination meditation.

> Reestablish your silent illumination meditation practice (described on pages 141–142).

> Continue with the meditation as your body/mind merge, inside/outside merge, and awareness opens to a vast, unbounded spaciousness. Rest in the merged field of awareness and the space holding vast awareness for an hour or more without serious interruption.

> Allow your awareness to shift slightly to the consciousness holding vast, unbounded space. It is vast, unbounded consciousness.

> Allow awareness to merge with vast, unbounded consciousness. Rest in the field of awareness merged with the unbounded consciousness containing vast, unbounded space for an hour or more without serious interruption.

> Now allow your awareness to shift slightly
> to the no-thing-ness, the absence quality hold-
> ing vast, unbounded consciousness. It is not
> a negative absence. There is nothing missing.
> It has a felt sense of a fullness, a fullness of
> Absence. It is the energy collating right before
> something that is not yet in existence comes
> into being—a kind of pregnant field ripe for
> the appearance of new life. It, too, is vast and
> unbounded.

> Allow awareness to merge with vast,
> unbounded no-thing-ness. Rest in the field
> of awareness merged with the unbounded
> no-thing-ness containing vast, unbounded
> consciousness for an hour or more without
> serious interruption.

The Eighth Jhāna:
The Base of Neither Perception
nor Non-perception

This is the realm that is most confounding to our conceptual mind. Exhibiting neither perception nor non-perception, it challenges our mind as it removes every concept, even the concept of no concept. We abide in this realm without mentally holding it as all concepts are nonexistent here. This is a realm of immediate and direct experience without an ability to conceptualize the realm, our awareness, or any experience here. Yet there is full awake awareness and intuitive knowing abiding in this realm.

This realm is very refined to experience. It is only known through direct experience abiding as Beingness with all possible concepts removed. Even the concept of removing concepts is absent from this realm. All forms of identity have a root in concept. Part of the reality of the everyday world is held together as real by the concepts we hold most dear. In the experience of this realm all concepts, including the concept of having no concept, is absent. There is nothing for our consciousness to hold or land upon. Each place we could land and each relational understanding we could have is absent. We must simply rest in awareness of this delicately subtle realm.

I recall being in this realm while on the two-month retreat I did with my teacher, the Venerable Pa Auk Sayadaw. I became so energetically sensitive that I had trouble using the same serving spoon as the other retreatants in the meal line. The felt perception of their energy on the serving spoon was nearly overwhelming to me. My sensitivity to the everyday world revealed the purity of the nearby Absolute realm. Part of what needed purification with the Base of Neither Perception nor Non-perception was my preference for absence, for formlessness. My consciousness needed to deeply know that absence, formlessness, and the profound peace of Cessation were not more desirable than the world of form, self-identity, and desire.

This is the first realm as the Absolute realm moves toward creation in form. It is a subtle step from the profound, still, pure love of the Absolute realm and the deep absence of all concepts, all forms, all formlessness in the experience of Cessation.

Neither Perception nor Non-perception Practice

There are a number of practices or meditations that can open awareness to the vast, unbounded quality of neither perception nor non-perception. Here I present one approach using silent illumination meditation.

> Reestablish your silent illumination meditation practice (described on pages 141–142).

> Continue with the meditation as your body/mind merge, inside/outside merge, and awareness opens to a vast, unbounded spaciousness. Rest in the merged field of awareness and the space holding vast awareness for an hour or more without serious interruption.

> Allow your awareness to shift slightly to the consciousness holding vast, unbounded space. It is perceived by vast, unbounded consciousness.

> Allow awareness to merge with vast, unbounded consciousness. Rest in the field

of awareness merged with the unbounded
consciousness containing vast, unbounded
space for an hour or more without serious
interruption.

> Allow your awareness to shift slightly to vast,
unbounded no-thing-ness—also called Absence.
Allow your awareness to merge with vast,
unbounded no-thing-ness. Rest in the field of
awareness merged with the absence quality
in unbounded no-thing-ness containing or
holding vast, unbounded consciousness for an
hour or more without serious interruption.

> Now allow your awareness to shift slightly to
the delicate, phenomenally subtle field that
contains or holds vast, unbounded no-thing-
ness. This is a field that is before any concept
or any absence of concept. This is direct
experience without the presence or absence of
meaning. It feels to be a vast field that defies
understanding other than through the direct
experience of merging with it.

> Allow awareness to merge with the vast,
unbounded nonconceptual field of awareness.

Rest in the field of awareness merged with the vast, unbounded nonconceptual realm, which is holding vast, unbounded no-thing-ness, for an hour or more without serious interruption.

The Ninth Jhāna:
Absolute Realm of Reality

The Absolute is the source of all creation and manifestation of tangible reality. It is a realm that is beyond any concept, idea, or projection about its qualities. The Absolute is awake and aware. It is a peacefulness containing a luminous loving radiance with profound presence. It feels graceful, poetic, and utterly complete in every way. When merged with the Absolute, there is no urge to go anywhere else or do anything else. Merged awareness with the Absolute is complete in itself. The Absolute is the beginning and end of all reality. It has no preferences, no favorites, no one religion or realization that best represents the totality of its Beingness.

Although there is neither exactly a quantifiable location nor a measure of time to the Absolute, it can be contacted and merged with in this moment of now. There is no time nor any other location than the Absolute. It is always here and always in the moment of now.

Despite there being no center, no hereness, to the Absolute, the felt sense is that personal awareness is merging with the Absolute the way shadow moves into darkness at night. When personal awareness is merging with the Absolute, that merged awareness can have a sense of being drawn deeper and deeper into the Absolute. This is evidenced by a loss of body perception, then thoughts slow to a stop, inner sensation quiets, and any knowing evaporates. At some point in this timeless time, all awareness and all consciousness cease into a profound Absence.

The Absolute feels graceful, poetic,
and utterly complete in every way.

As our refined awareness begins to approach the Ninth *Jhāna*, the Absolute realm, one psychological or self-identity issue that customarily arises is fear of extinction—the fear that we will cease to be the familiar self-identity with a life memory, familiar thought patterns, and a particular manner of being in our lives.

In meditation, like life itself, we need to approach difficult and scary possibilities slowly. We start by approaching whatever triggers our fear and stop when it feels to be too much for us to manage. We retreat or end the meditation at that point. It can be skillful to be maintaining both the innate goodness meditation and the silent illumination meditation as our awareness and consciousness approach the Ninth *Jhāna*. By repeatedly approaching the Absolute realm while staying with our fear of vanishing entirely, we defuse the energy of fear. We consistently see that nothing bad has happened. This gives us increasing confidence in our journey. (This would be the practice regardless of the fear, worry, anxiety, or terror that one might be experiencing.)

It is also advisable to be working with a teacher skilled in these *jhānas* and Awakening experiences. They can reassure us through their direction and presence that we are safe and on a journey many have done before us. In time, our fears subside and we are left with a deep curiosity about Absolute truth. What will it be like to completely merge into the Absolute realm?

I recall my first journey into the Absolute realm. As consciousness and awareness were merging with the pure, all-accepting love of the Absolute realm, I wondered if I would return. The love and Presence of Beingness were so strong and penetratingly comfortable that I found I dropped the preference to return. If awareness and consciousness fully merged with the Absolute realm and there was no separation of consciousness later, I was fine with that result. That is what embracing and loving the Absolute realm is like in direct experience.

Absolute Realm of Reality Practice

There are a number of practices or meditations that can open awareness to the vast, unbounded source. Here I present one approach using silent illumination meditation.

> Reestablish your silent illumination meditation practice (described on pages 141–142).

> Continue with the meditation as your body/mind merge, inside/outside merge, and awareness opens to a vast, unbounded spaciousness. Rest in the merged field of awareness and the space holding vast awareness for an hour or more without serious interruption.

> Allow your awareness to shift slightly to the consciousness holding vast, unbounded space. It is vast, unbounded consciousness.

> Allow awareness to merge with vast, unbounded consciousness. Rest in the field of awareness merged with the unbounded consciousness containing vast, unbounded

space for an hour or more without serious interruption.

> Allow your awareness to shift slightly to vast, unbounded no-thing-ness.

> Allow awareness to merge with vast, unbounded no-thing-ness. Rest in the field of awareness merged with the unbounded no-thing-ness containing or holding vast, unbounded consciousness for an hour or more without serious interruption.

> Now allow your awareness to shift slightly to the delicate, phenomenally subtle field that contains or holds vast, unbounded no-thing-ness. This is a field that is before any concept or any absence of concept. This is direct experience without the presence or absence of meaning. It feels to be a vast field that defies understanding other than through the direct experience of merging with it.

> Allow awareness to merge with the vast, unbounded nonconceptual field of awareness. Rest in the field of awareness merged with the vast, unbounded nonconceptual realm, which

is holding vast, unbounded no-thing-ness, for an hour or more without serious interruption.

> Open awareness to the presence quality of that which is the source of the animating life force of pure love and pure presence. There will be a particular felt sense at the source of all reality. It is the felt sense of Beingness itself at its origin. The Absolute realm is a combination of pure love, pure awareness, and pure Beingness/Presence. We can call the pure Beingness pure Presence. It is the purest love you can ever directly experience. The pure love will draw awareness into its field. The love is so intensely loving and accepting that it absorbs everything that is met.

> Allow awareness to be drawn in and absorbed in the pure love, pure awareness, and pure presence of the Absolute realm. Rest in the merged pure awareness, pure presence, and pure love for an hour or more without serious interruption.

Should the Absolute realm draw your nonlocalized, objective awareness deeper in the powerful field of complete, all-accepting love, there will be no sense of having any location. All perception of being any form of materiality is gone. All perception of being any mental functioning, thoughts, concepts, or ideas quiets to the point that all quality or function of mentality is gone. Finally, with the arising and complete merging with the source of Absolute reality, consciousness stops. This direct experience is called Cessation. Cessation ends when our consciousness restarts in the Absolute realm. It restarts with the felt sense of the impact of Cessation and with knowing that there is fruit arising from the experience of Cessation. This is called *nirodha samādhi* in Buddhism.

Vajra (Diamondlike) Body

When Cessation is an open portal to the individual consciousness, there can be an activation of the *Vajra* body. The *Vajra* body is a diamondlike, luminous body that contains all realizations and Awakenings that have been experienced in that particular consciousness. It is called the diamondlike body because it cannot be destroyed. It is not born, nor does it ever die. It is a clear, faceted substance.

In the *Nirvāṇa Sutra*, an important Mahayana Buddhist text, the Buddha says, "The *tathāgata* body is a body and is not a body. It was not born and it will not cease to exist. It is immeasurable and boundless. It is utterly pure."

I also call the *Vajra* body a vehicle because it has the sense of being self-contained, with inherent wisdom and the potential to timelessly journey toward the deepest truth. There are many facets of knowing and points of clarity of realization in the *Vajra* body, as well as a distilled core quality of the host consciousness. That is, it contains our essential flavor as a particular individual—our core personal essence is a part of its construction and radiance. In my experience there was a sweetness that was the distillation of my heart. It was particular and unique to my deepest heart qualities. This gave the *Vajra* body a subtle sweetness to its nature.

Although I had first realized the *Vajra* body with two of my teachers a few years earlier, my most transformative experience of it occurred one crisp fall morning in 2018 while I was also having a stroke. A deep realization began unfolding.

I had been preparing to leave for the airport to fly to attend a retreat. Suddenly, my vision became completed blurred. I could not see anything clearly. I felt mentally confused, profoundly confused, with the worst head pain of my life. As the completely blurred vision continued, I found my awareness gravitated to a clear contained space right outside the back of my head. It was a little to the right of my spinal cord.

Resting with open awareness in this clear space, I could feel contact with the different Awakenings and realizations that had occurred in my particular consciousness. It was an awareness of awakeness. In this loving space, awareness was relaxed and curious. I became clear that if my body died, this contained, clear space would be a kind of vehicle for awareness and consciousness to journey from this particular lifetime elsewhere. This clear space vehicle encapsulated all realizations up to this point. It was independent of my life and my history. I could sense the individual particularities that made up my life, which would fall away upon death.

When the stroke commenced, I decided to lie down and rest. After about an hour, my vision cleared enough to see. Because I thought that it was a vision problem, I elected to go to a local urgent care facility. I was later transferred to a local hospital and a stroke was confirmed through testing. Almost three years later, I have nearly fully recovered from the stroke. There are some body limitations I carry still.

Since that stroke the clear space of realization has remained. The knowing that there is an aware vehicle that will journey to the next lifetime gives me comfort. Merging with the Absolute or another lifetime with this clear awareness always present touches my heart with its peacefulness. I do not wonder what will happen when this life ends. I do not lament what an afterlife will hold.

> *The knowing that there is an aware vehicle that will journey to the next lifetime gives me comfort. . . . I do not wonder what will happen when this life ends. I do not lament what an afterlife will hold.*

The *Vajra* body is a vehicle that would leave this body possibly to be reborn or perhaps to simply and naturally rejoin the Absolute realm, resting in the merged, undifferentiated state of indescribable beauty, rapt poetry of living, and deeply fulfilling love.

My perception was that, upon the death of the human body hosting the *Vajra* body, the *Vajra* body can either enter the experience of Cessation abiding in its majestic depths or it can be reborn into the world, possibly guiding others to realize their undivided, united connection with the Absolute through profound teachings, meditations, and practices. My contact and realization of the *Vajra* body convinced me that its primary function is to hold all realizations and experiences of Awakening for the next rebirth, the next human lifetime. I was able to confirm the experience of the *Vajra* body with two of my teachers.

In Tibetan Buddhist tradition, the high lamas—such as the Dalai Lama, the Panchen Lama, and the Karmapa—all are reincarnated. The balance of Buddhism believes in rebirth rather than reincarnation. The difference between the two is whether the collection of realizations and Awakenings is collected, packaged, for the next lifetime; in reincarnation, it is, whereas in rebirth, it is not.

It makes some sense that if this current lifetime contained a significant number of realizations and Awakenings, humanity—and Beingness itself—would greatly benefit from those realizations being readily accessible in the next lifetime. Beingness, appearing as worldwide humanity, would be able to continue on a spiritual path towards deepening Awakening, towards fully functioning as the Absolute realm in human form.

If you are called and ready to heed the call home, start with the foundational meditations here, particularly the innate goodness meditation. Let your heart be touched and impacted by these meditations. Begin your spiritual journal and start to observe your own mind and actions. See what feels incongruent and investigate its history. In doing both the meditations and observing behavior, you will refine your history and how that history impacts you today. When the experience of absence of self arises, stay with it. Do not feel a need to solve the absence of self's uncertainties. Stay with the not-knowing. Remain open to the flowering of Awakening of *kenshō* within the experience of consciousness. Awakening can and will flower in the ripeness of time.

Conclusion

IN THIS BOOK, we have traversed from the beginning of a spiritual meditative path into the territory of First Awakening and beyond, working with customary resistances to a First Awakening, the natural embodiment processes, and advanced practices through final realization and the ceasing of the normal self-identity. Additionally, we have explored the realization and manifestation of the *Vajra* or diamond-like body of consciousness, awareness, and realization.

Each of us can know, and more importantly function as, our true nature. We can reveal and change deep-seated behavior, and we can then progressively open to the deeper realities of the universe as these are realized within a particular consciousness.

If you are one of the millions called to return home, these practices are for you. None of us know what Awakenings or realizations may be in store for us. Yet the journey of absence of self, unity experiences of love, the different levels and depths of Awakening, deepening self-realizations, discovery, and investigation of our personal material and behavior— they all invite and challenge us to continuously live from the deepest truth of reality as we know it. Knowing a deep truth is helpful. Yet it is when we can embody realization and live from it that our life becomes alive and imbued with and as true nature.

On this breathtaking path of realization of reality, we need a sure-footed guide to demonstrate how to traverse this unfamiliar landscape, a teacher who can support us where we are while gently pointing slightly ahead on the trail: "Look there. The view is breathtaking." In time we each learn that the "there" our teacher points to is really right here, right now, as it always has been and always will be.

Now is the time to start your journey home.

Acknowledgments

I FEEL PROFOUND GRATITUDE to each and all of my teachers. Their example and guidance have been invaluable in pointing the way.

A special thank-you to the team who took this book from my first manuscript to the amazing book it has become—Carra Simpson, Erin Parker, Jazmin Welch, and Lynn Slobogian.

Finally, thank you to each of my students. Your embracing of the teachings and practices, along with your penetrating questions and shining examples, has helped me clarify and refine my teaching.

Glossary

absence of self: The experience of the customary self-identity being increasingly transparent and difficult to locate within.

Absolute: The source of all life animation, all form, and formless reality.

Absolute realm: The realm where the Absolute can be directly and deeply perceived, experienced, and merged with.

accordion effect: Whenever awareness expands to a new level, the self-identity generally reacts shortly thereafter by contracting as tightly as possible.

adhiṭṭhāna: Resolve; intention. One of the *pāramīs/* perfections of Buddhism.

ānāpānasati: Breath awareness meditation; from the Pali *ānāpāna* (breath) and *sati* (awareness).

arahant: The highest level, fourth stage of Awakening in the Theravada Buddhist tradition.

awareness: Perception, with or without consciousness, of internal and external events unfolding.

Beingness: Unconditioned presence.

***bodhisattva*:** A Mahayana Buddhist ideal in which one forgoes full enlightenment, over countless lifetimes, until all beings are awake.

Buddha nature: The inherent potential of each being to be fully awake and fully realized.

Cessation: The experience of complete merging into the pure love, pure presence, and pure Beingness of the Absolute realm, in which all mentality and materiality ceases. Another name for a potential enlightenment experience (i.e., there may be experiential changes following Cessation that permanently change the self-identity, including an Awakening experience).

Chan: The Chinese Buddhist tradition of using *kung-an/kōan* and silent illumination meditation/*shikantaza* to open and directly experience Cessation and likely an Awakening experience.

concentration meditation: A collection of meditations in which the meditator stays with one meditative object to the exclusion of all other sense data or experience.

consciousness: Awareness coupled with ordinary and intuitive knowing.

crystal body: The meditative fruit of practicing four elements meditation in which the meditator experiences their physical body as a crystal body.

Daigo-tettei: The third level of Awakening experience (*kenshō*) in the Zen tradition, in which the self-identity drops away and is not reactivated again.

dāna: Generosity of heart; reciprocal generosity. One of the *pāramīs*/perfections of Buddhism.

dhamma/dharma: Teaching or universal law.

dual unity: A state where the infant is in a nondifferentiated state of individuation and is thus in a union with all other beings until the self-identity lands in the individual consciousness.

dukkha: The first noble truth of Buddhism that human life contains dissatisfactoriness/suffering.

ekaggatā: The *jhāna* factor of one-pointedness.

eternal now: The true measure of time, as the past and future are concepts only.

felt sense: Intuitive perception of what is not visually apparent.

First Awakening: An Awakening experience that contains (1) a deep experience of absence of self, (2) clear seeing of one's true nature as one's true identity, and (3) a thorough unity experience where all is one or everything is a fabric of Oneness.

four elements meditation: A practice deconstructing earth, water, fire, and wind, the elements of physical reality.

four stages of Awakening: The Theravada Buddhist map of Awakening. The first stage is stream entry, the second stage is once-returner, the third stage is non-returner, and the fourth stage is *arahant*.

gradual cultivation: An ongoing spiritual practice that slowly erodes the firm conviction in each of us being a separate self while concurrently opening to transcendent/ Awakening experiences.

innate goodness: The inherent quality of our true nature; goodness not dependent on any manner of doing or way of being.

jhāna: The third level of concentration, also called absorption concentration; a nondual state with no discernible self, complete awareness, and no thoughts.

jhāna **factors:** Available in all meditations; (1) applied awareness, (2) sustained awareness, (3) joy, (4) bliss, and (5) one-pointedness.

kalāpa(s): Subatomic particles of conditioned reality.

kenshō: Seeing into one's true nature; from Zen tradition map of Awakening.

khanti: Patience; forbearance. One of the *pāramīs*/perfections of Buddhism.

kōan: A spiritual paradox that cannot be resolved by the thinking mind; spiritual intuition and realization offer the perfect solution.

levels of concentration: (1) Momentary concentration, (2) access concentration, and (3) absorption concentration/ *jhāna*.

māra: The impediments to Awakening and realizations.

nekkhamma: Renunciation. One of the *pāramīs*/perfections of Buddhism.

nibbāna/nirvāṇa: An experience of Cessation in which all materiality and mentality cease.

nirodha/Cessation: An experience in which all materiality and mentality cease, including consciousness and awareness.

no-self: An experience in which the customary self-identity is absent (or transparent) and a unity experience of all is one is concurrently present.

non-returner: The third stage of Awakening in Theravada Buddhist tradition.

once-returner: The second stage of Awakening in Theravada Buddhist tradition.

paññā: Wisdom. One of the *pāramīs*/perfections of Buddhism.

pāramīs/**perfections:** The qualities Buddhists are encouraged to develop during their lifetime: (1) generosity/*dāna*, (2) wholesomeness/*sīla*, (3) renunciation/*nekkhamma*, (4) wisdom/*paññā*, (5) energy/*vīriya*, (6) patience/*khanti*, (7) truthfulness/*sacca*, (8) resolve/*adhiṭṭhāna*, (9) loving-kindness/*mettā*, and (10) equanimity/*upekkhā.*

pīti: The *jhāna* factor of joy, possibly rapturous joy.

presence: Experiential contact with the Beingness quality of this present moment.

realm: A location of reality that is perceived to be outside ordinary reality.

resistances: Psychological or emotional patterns of mind or behavior that restrict awareness from contacting qualities of our true nature, including a First Awakening.

sacca: Truthfulness. One of the *pāramīs*/perfections of Buddhism.

satori: The sustained *kenshō* experience of seeing into one's true nature. In *satori* the experience is both more far-reaching and sustaining than *kenshō*.

self-identity: The psychological patterns of mind and behavior that define who we are to ourselves; self-concept; self-recognition. *Satori* will awaken in 51 percent or more of consciousness for a shift in identity from the customary personality view to true nature.

shikantaza: The Japanese name for silent illumination meditation.

sīla: Wholesomeness/virtue. One of the *pāramīs*/perfections of Buddhism.

silent illumination meditation: The Chinese Chan Buddhist meditation of being awareness to unify (1) body/mind, (2) inside/outside, and (3) vastness without conceptual boundaries.

skandhas: Form, feeling, perception, impulses, and consciousness; the Buddhist definition of how a self is composed.

stream entry: The first stage of Awakening in Theravada Buddhist tradition.

sukha: The *jhāna* factor of bliss.

suttas (Pali)/*sutras* (Sanskrit): A sermon or religious talk offered by Shakyamuni Buddha.

tathāgatagarba: The seed of Tathāgata (Buddha, one who is in this world but not of this world).

Theravada Buddhism: The tradition of Buddhism maintaining the traditional meditative practices of the Buddha.

true nature: The true, core foundation of unconditioned reality.

Vajra **body:** An experience that awakens a portion of consciousness preserving all realizations and Awakening experiences to survive after death of the body.

vicāra: The *jhāna* factor of sustained awareness or attention.

vīriya: Energy. One of the *pāramīs*/perfections of Buddhism.

vitakka: The *jhāna* factor of applied awareness or attention.

Zen Buddhism: The Buddhist tradition evolving from Chinese Chan Buddhism in which Awakening is the primary objective.

About the Author

STEPHEN SNYDER began practicing daily meditation in 1976. Since then, he has studied Buddhism extensively—investigating and engaging in Zen, Tibetan, Theravada, and Western non-dual traditions. Stephen was authorized to teach in 2007 by the Venerable Pa Auk Sayadaw, a Burmese meditation 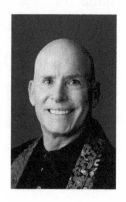 master and renowned scholar. In 2009, he coauthored *Practicing the Jhānas*, exploring concentration meditation as presented by Pa Auk Sayadaw.

Stephen's resonant and warmhearted teaching style engages students around the globe through in-person and online retreats, as well as one-on-one coaching. He encourages students to turn toward awakened awareness and, through this realizing, embody their true identity. Stephen is also author of *Stress Reduction for Lawyers, Law Students, and Legal Professionals* and *Buddha's Heart*. For more information, please visit awakeningdharma.org.

Did you benefit from
Demystifying Awakening?

SHARE YOUR PRAISE

Did this book help you to develop your personal meditation practice? Did it offer new insights into Buddhist teachings that are benefiting your daily life or interactions? If so, a review shared through your favorite online retailer would be warmly welcomed. A few minutes of your time could help others find this book and benefit as you have.

PLACE A BULK ORDER

Would you like to share this book with a group or a class? Please be in touch! We can offer bulk discounts for orders of ten or more copies to most locations. Please write to buddhasheartpress@gmail.com.

KEEP IN TOUCH

For more about Stephen's books, workshops, and other offerings, please visit awakeningdharma.org.

Also by Stephen Snyder

Buddha's Heart: Meditation Practice for Developing Well-Being, Love, and Empathy
PAPERBACK • 978-1-7347810-2-1 • $16.95
E-BOOK • 978-1-7347810-3-8 • $9.95
PUBLISHED NOVEMBER 2020

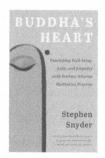

An original and clear path to the powerful *brahmavihāras*—ancient Buddhist heart practices. These practices offer rich, soothing support for the soul and a portal to spiritual awakening and deepening self-realization. *Buddha's Heart* teaches what seems counterintuitive but is undeniably true: the more we open our hearts, the more resilient and flexible we are. And the more authentically vulnerable we are, the safer and more protected we become.

Stress Reduction for Lawyers, Law Students, and Legal Professionals: Learning to Relax
PAPERBACK • 978-1-7347810-0-7 • $14.95
E-BOOK • 978-1-7347810-1-4 • $9.95
PUBLISHED SEPTEMBER 2020

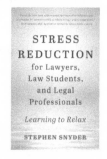

A practical guide for a more relaxed and enjoyable legal career—authored by a retired lawyer and senior meditation teacher. This book offers straightforward techniques to identify the events that cause stress in your work, apply practices that support deep relaxation, and develop greater satisfaction in your work and personal life.

Practicing the Jhānas: Traditional Concentration Meditation as Presented by the Venerable Pa Auk Sayadaw
PAPERBACK • 978-1-59030-733-5 • $22.95
E-BOOK • 978-0-8348-2282-5 • $17.99
PUBLISHED DECEMBER 2009
COAUTHORED WITH TINA RASMUSSEN

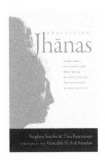

A clear and in-depth presentation of the traditional Theravada concentration meditation known as *jhāna* practice, developed from practicing *jhāna* meditation in retreat under the guidance of one of the great living meditation masters, the Venerable Pa Auk Sayadaw.

CPSIA information can be obtained
at www.ICGtesting.com
Printed in the USA
BVHW030216040123
655542BV00002B/29

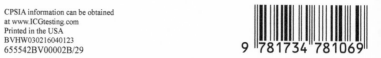